Torremolinos

An all-American kid's exile

in a 1950's Spanish seaside village

by David M. Johnson

Correspondence:
913 Fell Street
Baltimore, MD 21231
(917) 363-6707
derj490@aol.com

Published April 2016 in the United States
by Create Space a division of Amazon

First draft
Registered with Writer's Guild of America, East
February 13, 2006.Reg. # 136413

Final draft
Registered with Writer's Guild of America, East
January 19, 2016

ISBN – 13: 978-0692646571
ISBN - 10: 0692646574

Para España y los Españoles

Peter,

From one ex-pat
brat to another.

Saludos,

David

CONTENTS

PICTURE CREDITS
The pictures in this book come from two main sources;

1. Personal photo collections of the Johnson family and those generously shared by Nora Boren, who back then we knew as "Missy" Ericson.

2. Photos made available to the public on Wikimedia Commons under their Creative Commons Licensing.

The photos at the head of each chapter I have artistically blurred and altered to give the feeling of a time and place gone by remembered bit by bit, just as these memories came to me, like distant thunder. I hope you enjoy them.

1

Una Vacacion

I CAN SHOOT A HISSING POISONOUS COPPERHEAD right through his glaring yellow eyeball from 100 yards off. I can kill giant, slavering grizzly bears with just my bare hands and a gleaming Bowie knife.

I can outwrassle wild Indians, whole war-whooping tribes of them.

Then I can palaver with them in their own native tongues: Cree, Choctaw, Kiowa, you name it.

I am Davy Crockett, King of the Wild Frontier.

And there is nothing in these woods I need fear.

Actually, I am nine years old. I am standing in my front yard in suburban Chevy Chase, official Davy Crockett coonskin cap on, furry tail and all.

My mother has just told me a piece of news. Like the hardy frontiersman I am, I pay little heed to what the squaw just jabbered at me.

It does not seem like a biggie. Not to Davy Crockett.

Big news is more like the day my brother Mark comes running up Ridgewood Street to say Mom and Dad have put on a big fight, there has been screaming and a shower of plates and Dad drove off and isn't going to live with us anymore.

That is big, and puzzling news, the sort of stuff even mighty Davy Crockett thinks long and hard about before going back to the neighborhood game of Kick the Can.

Even then, just before you kick that 32 ounce Hawaiian Punch can and send it sailing into the yard of Billy Ronson (whose grandad beats him in their next door house nightly with a belt as you cringe in the yard and hear him yell in pain with each whack) you wonder what life without Dad is going to be like.

And why did Mom throw plates at him anyway?

Or, big news is like the time when Dad is still there, before he becomes "the guy who takes you out on Sunday," and he looks up from the Washington Post with a huff of exclamation and an announcement.

"I'll be darned. It says the locusts are coming. They were in the Carolinas Thursday, massive swarms of them. And they'll be here tomorrow."

And you aren't quite sure what locusts are but they must be big news. They're in the Post. And they only show up every 23 years, so, yes, it's a big deal.

The next day, everywhere is covered with these big brown-winged insects. Sort of like fat crickets, only brown not green, and kind of insect ugly somehow. They're on trees, bushes, sidewalks, roofs, cars, everything.

As you walk to your friend Petey Wechsler's house you have to squish them under your feet so your every step is punctuated by a gooshey locusty echo.

Step. "Squish!"

Step. "Splooch!"

Step. "Squinch!"

To Davy Crockett, they make a mighty satisfying crunch.

The locusts, now that's news.

Instead, what my mother has mistakenly presented as news seems just some casual chatter to Davy Crockett as he surveys his wild domain, in an untamed frontier territory called Bethesda, Maryland.

It is something about going to spend the summer at the beach in some place called "Spain," and maybe leaving school a little early to go there. No big deal. I mean, we've been to "Rehoboth Beach" and "Nags Head," how different can a beach in someplace called "Spain" possibly be?

When you're a kid, you just sort of nod and accept things like this. You don't worry and fret about it for long, not if you're reasonably confident you're going to be fed and clothed and such.

And besides, and this is the real killer point, there's nothing much you can do about it, even if you are King of the Wild Frontier. The grownups hold all the cards; you're just sort of a passenger on their ship.

And this particular ship has turned hard a port and headed for someplace called Spain.

Okay, fine, Squaw Woman. We will do as you say, at least for now.

So as a scrawny nine-year-old fourth grader in Chevy Chase, Maryland, I accept the fact I will be spending the summer in some country I think I'd only heard of in a Disney cartoon about Ferdinand the Friendly Bull.

I sort of picture Spain as a cross between this cartoon and a sandy beach where I will take my ball, mitt and bat and teach the Spanish kids to play baseball. Maybe I will even let them wear my coonskin cap.

Fortunately, I am blissfully oblivious of the fact I won't see America or my father for years, that I won't return to live in the States till I am nineteen, and that by then I will become enough of an expatriate that I will feel like a stranger on a strange planet, some kind of goonish crypto-Spaniard: part Gringo, part Spic, like one of those sci-fi half-man, half-machine things that fits in nowhere and in the end must be destroyed for the good of all mankind.

That's later.

At the time I'm just your average American, snot-nosed, little nincompoop kid. You know, cub scouts, Pack 255 ("the greatest pack alive"), as opposed to my brother's Pack 256 (He claims their motto is "we've got bigger dicks"). I watch Howdy Doody and The Mickey Mouse Club on TV and have a thing for Darlene (I never understand the whole fuss about Annette Funicello: she never does it for me. Darlene's my girl.)

I'm in fourth grade at Rosemary Elementary School in the Chevy Chase, Maryland, suburb of Washington, D.C. Every morning I pledge allegiance to the flag of the United States of America, one nation invisible.

We're supposed to mindlessly say "indivisible" but that word makes zero sense to me, so "invisible" America is. Later kids have to say "under God" (this was before Madeline Murray and the whole prayer thing).

I am pretty much the whole nine yards: the all-American boy, born in the nation's capital, ready and willing and able to grow up, go to BCC, Bethesda-Chevy Chase High School in Bethesda, Maryland, and become another shining American success story.

Early this year, I watch a local friend's brother play at BCC as quarterback and see him score a touchdown as his pretty cheerleader girlfriend waves her big pom-poms at him, then plants a hug and kiss on him. The packed bleachers roar and the school band plays a victory hurrah.

I tell myself: "Yes, sir! Sign me up for this!"

Be a high school star in football and baseball, have a pretty cheerleader girlfriend with big pom-poms and the whole shebang.

And just plain be Joe America. Yessir.

No way, José.

It seems like no time later, I'm standing with my older brother, Mark, and little sister, Mimi, watching the pale green statue of Liberty fade into the misty spring air of 1957.

We are headed out of New York harbor on the decks of the large *Cristoforo Columbo,* an Italian line ship. Mark has already gotten seasick and hurled the goodbye lunch we had in Chinatown into the flat dull-green waters of the Hudson River.

While we are at least momentarily a little stunned at the prospect of seeing America recede further and further away from us, we're secretly thrilled to be on this particular ship: because it is the sister ship of the ill-fated *Andrea Doria.*

This sends chills of excitement coursing through our little bodies, goose bumps on our scrawny kid arms.

We remember.

Cut to a year earlier, we listen to the Andrea Doria's grim fate with rapt attention on a car radio. We are driving down from a vacation in Canada and we keep the radio on.

All over America people are glued to their TV's and radios to hear the latest details of a story that sweeps Dwight Eisenhower's re-election campaign and the Suez Canal crisis from the headlines.

The *Andrea Doria* is the *Titanic* of 1956. And we are practically there for the whole saga of this ship, at least on a car radio and in the newspaper photos.

She is built in 1951 to restore Italian cruise ships to prominence (all the big ones had apparently been sunk in World War II).

The *Andrea Doria* is quickly nicknamed "The Grand Dame of the Sea". Like the *Titanic* (and the nearly identical *Cristoforo Colombo* we are sailing to Spain on) she is billed as one of the safest ships of her time with eleven watertight compartments and modern radar to warn of collisions.

In true Italian style and comfort she has completed 100 crossings of the Atlantic secure and safe.

Crossing number 101 doesn't go the same.

Off the island of Nantucket the *Andrea Doria* runs into dense fog.

She gets on a collision course with a large Swedish-American liner, the *Stockholm,* which happens to have a sturdy steel bow re-enforced to break ice.

Inquiries later show that the *Andrea Doria's* Italian crew is not following the right radar procedure. When they realize a collision is imminent, they should follow international protocol for a head-on crossing at sea; both ships must turn hard right to avoid a collision between them.

The Swedes turn hard right.

The Italians turn left.

Dead smack into the path of the onrushing steel bow of the *Stockholm.*

At 11:10 p.m., in the fog and the night, the steel-hard ice-breaking ram of the Stockholm chews into the *Andrea Doria's* starboard side so hard it devours nearly forty feet crushing three cabin decks full of sleeping people.

Most of the 51 who die are killed instantly, crushed by the Stockholm's relentless prow.

The *Andrea Doria* survives just a little bit longer herself.

Quickly, her empty starboard fuel tanks flood and the Grand Dame of the Sea lists over 20 degrees. This not only floods the non-watertight upper decks, it makes her list further, rendering half her lifeboats useless.

The crew and passengers are suddenly in real mortal peril. There won't be enough lifeboats for everybody.

Since the blow to her bow sent her anchors to the ocean floor, the *Stockholm* is literally chained there to the sea bottom and takes part in the rescue. So does the legendary ocean liner the *Ile de France* which appears out of the Nantucket sea mist like a ghost ship from the storied past to lend its lifeboats.

Passengers on the *Stockholm* are surprised to see that the first lifeboats that flee over from the *Andrea Doria* do not contain women and children or any passengers at all. Instead the precious lifeboats are full of the *Andrea Doria's* working staff: the waiters and cabin stewards who scrambled into the boats first, leaving the passengers to fend for themselves.

At 6:05 a.m. on July 26 the last of the passengers and crew are safely taken off.

At 10:09 a.m., barely ten hours after the collision, the *Andrea Doria* rolls and slips under the waves. She goes down in 225 feet of water.

We follow all of this on the tinny car radio, getting reports of the sinking as it happens. Later it's in all the newspapers and magazines. Life magazine puts out a special story with tons of harrowing pictures.

The unlucky *Andrea Doria* is news as big as it gets.

And now, on our way to Spain, we are standing on the very ominous decks of its sister ship.

As we embark to Spain on the *Andrea Doria's* near carbon copy, it sends a little thrill of excitement shooting up our childish backs.

Mark, Mimi and I are convinced that we, too, might enjoy a daring shipwreck. When the crew stages a lifeboat drill and we don our bright orange life jackets, we are certain any night now it may be our turn to rush to the lifeboats for real.

It's a deliciously exciting idea. To paraphrase 1950's TV host Art Linkletter "kids think the darndest things."

Before bedding down for the night, we mull it over, smiling at the idea. Will the sister ship's curse be visited upon the liner we're on, will we be shipwrecked and live forever as castaways?

Yes and no.

The *Cristoforo Colombo* drops us off uneventfully in Algeciras harbor, well within sight of the towering rock of Gibraltar, and later steams safely off to Genoa. It is retired from the New York run in 1973 and is used for years for less and less glorious service. It is never shipwrecked, just finally scrapped in Taiwan in 1982.

But we, the three Johnson kids from Chevy Chase, USA, we are shipwrecked in another sense of the word.

We get off in a dusty Spanish port city and take a dilapidated bus, gears grinding, up the winding coast road the next day.

We are supposedly going to a town called Marbella but, when this place appears from the bus too noisy, dusty and poor, my mother freaks. She pushes us back on the bus and we end up quite by chance in a place called Torremolinos.

Though we are unaware of it, we will be marooned here thousands of miles from any sort of civilization as we know it.

In Spain there is no Davy Crockett. No wild frontier. No coonskin caps. No football or pom-pom-waving cheerleaders in our futures, no cheering bleachers or happy high school bands.

Our world, as we know it, is gone.

This is something that will only dawn on us bit by bit.

We also don't appreciate the fleeting glimpse we will get at a very special place in time, in the soul of Spain, of a simple village way of life that will soon vanish from that seacoast forever as completely as the *Andrea Doria* disappeared into the cold, uncaring waters of the Atlantic.

Like I said, I'm oblivious of this at the time.

All I know is that Davy Crockett might know how to handle an untamed Tennessee frontier, and wrest a living from the good land of America, and speak the wild Indian languages.

But, here on this totally foreign soil, he's as helpless as Superman in the presence of Kryptonite.

There are no familiar forests, no raccoon, no grizzly bears to wrasse. And the natives don't speak Cree or Seminole or even Kiowa.

Instead they palaver in an incomprehensible babble of a tongue called "Spanish".

All Davy Crockett can do is look around befuddled and say:

"No comprendo."

David M. Johnson

2
Bienvenidos

IT'S BEEN MAYBE THREE WEEKS since we arrived. We have moved out of the small pink Hotel Flores on the coastal *carretera.*

My mother has found us a new temporary home in a summerhouse on a gentle slope above town called the *Cuesta de los Lomos.*

It will be the first of many homes we occupy during the four years we are in this part of this world. It's above the place in the *carretera* where the machine-gun toting Guardia Civil have their home barracks, right near where the railway crosses the highway and wends its way west towards Fuengirola.

We are beginning to know our way around the place, to feel a little like we belong in this unfamiliar land, to actually begin to recognize a few local kids.

As my mother and Mimi do some shopping in one of the small grocery stores, Mark and I amble up and down the Calle San Miguel, the main street, with an American kid we have met named Mackey. Briefly, Mark and Mackey walk off somewhere.

I am petting one of the bush-laden donkey's outside the bakery, talking to him to reassure him he's indeed a handsome little animal, a prince among the long-eared fraternity. I turn to head down the street to rejoin my companions.

Someone blocks my way.

I look up to see a Spanish kid, bigger and older than I am, maybe thirteen or fourteen, dressed in working man's blue cotton pants and a rough grey flannel shirt.

Maybe it's his close-cropped head with the scars on it, or the way he's standing with slightly clenched fists, or the look on his face, something makes me a just a little apprehensive. He smiles, but it's not exactly a friendly smile, and spits out a question that's not really a question.

"Americano, eh?"

I'm trying to decide whether to nod yes or just smile a bit and say *"si"*.... maybe he's just curious to know where I'm from, maybe he's merely starting a conversation to make friends, could be sort of trying to break the ice maybe...

Bam!

A jolt of hot, white light shoots through my eyes as his big fist lands smack on my jaw and I topple backwards, blood pouring from my nose.

The next thing I know I'm sitting on the cement of the street, rubbing tears from my eyes and shaking my head to free it of these noisy, spinning sensations. As I shakily get to my feet, white dots swimming in my eyeballs, I see the young Spaniard has blocked my brother's way and is asking him the same question

"Americano, eh?"

I start to yell out a warning.

"Hey, Mark, don't answer that question because...."

Wham!

Mark gets knocked on his rear end like I did, as the young Spaniard nods and grins malevolently back at us before moving off down the street, swaggering with his fists held out proudly to his sides.

As I help Mark up off the pavement, our new American friend Mackey comes up trying to staunch a bloody nose with his hand, thick red drops splattering onto his shirt and on the street.

"Th-this big kid just hit me for no reason."

We worriedly compare notes with little to conclude except that this bigger kid doesn't seem to like Americans very much, which doesn't bode well for us since we're American and smaller to boot. We're more than a little scared of him. As we're trying to decide on some plan of action, Mackey looks up with alarm.

"Look out! He's coming back!"

Indeed our tormentor is not only returning our way, he makes a beeline for us, and grabs Mark again by the shirt as he cocks his fist back.

"Americano, ya vas a ver!"

We all flinch in anticipation of the stinging blow.

It never lands.

Instead, the Spaniard flies magically backwards himself and lands sprawling on the pavement. I look at Mark in awe, wondering how he did that. He's just standing there as puzzled as I am.

Right next to him, fist still raised, is another Spanish kid, about the same age as the guy who's been hitting us, wearing a black beret at a rakish angle.

I know this guy from seeing him around town and at the beach with his herd of goats. He's known as *"El Carbonero"* because he also helps the local coal or *carbon*, vendor. Like the bully kid, he's dressed in a grey flannel shirt and blue cotton pants, though his are overalls.

"El Carbonero" looks sternly down at the bully kid lying shocked in the street and says something in Spanish.

"Quieres más?"

Sitting on his rear end in the street, the other kid looks up in alarm. He doesn't like whatever *"El Carbonero"* has said because he shakes his head "no." Then the bullyboy springs up and bolts away for dear life down the railroad track.

With a shout and gesture for us to follow, our rescuer sprints after him. We race to watch as he catches the fleeing kid maybe a hundred feet down the rail line, where a farmer's corn field grows opposite the station.

Like a swift hawk pouncing on a helpless rabbit, *"El Carbonero"* seizes his prey and hauls the screaming kid to the ground between the two rails. Whap! Whap! A couple of fists slam into the protesting Americano-hater as *"El Carbonero"* sits on him.

He whacks him about the head again. The bully-turned-victim cries out and tries to cover his head with his hands, wincing with each blow.

Whack!

"Ay!"

Whomp!

"Ay!"

I'm standing there, rubbing my sore jaw, kind of enjoying this show when *"El Carbonero"* looks up at me and holds out his victim by the shirt collar, motioning for me to smack him.

"Pégale. Anda, pégale!"

I shake my head "no," There's something in the kid's codebook against hitting someone who's actually being held down. Besides, I'm still kind of frightened by the shaven-headed guy, even in his current desperate situation.

One by one *"El Carbonero"* makes the same offer to Mark and to Mackey, whose nose has stopped bleeding.

Like me, they decline.

Having made his point, *"El Carbonero"* gives his victim a little warning that we surmise lets him know he's not to bother us again. Then the victor gets up and his punching bag boy runs away down the tracks crying for his mama.

"Ay, mi ma! ""Ay, mi ma!"

"El Carbonero" says something reassuring to us in Spanish, claps us on the shoulders, and walks off about his business, as if this was all in a day's work.

There are some interesting Spanish kids around. And now we're acquainted with two of them, or, in one case, with their angry fists.

"El Carbonero" we find out bit by bit is an all-around decent kid. He's about thirteen or fourteen and works two jobs to support his family, one as a goat herd, the other helping Señor Donkey Binky haul his coal around town.

I never ask him whether he goes to school or not; my guess is his family can't afford to send him. He's always there with a smile and a warm *"adios,"* And, at least in one case, with some protective fists.

The bullyboy who assaulted us, his name is Elias. Like *"El Carbonero"* he's also from a modest family. They live in a small blue railroad company house by the westernmost rail crossing.

His dad's job is to manually lower and raise the crossing gate, a job I'm told is reserved for railroad employees permanently injured on the job. They can't have much money from that, maybe that's why Elias is pissed off at us, spoiled tourist kids from what to him look like rich families.

Years later, when I see what tourism and people like us have done to this sweet village, I actually wonder for a while if the bully Elias somehow sensed what the future had in store for his little town.

Maybe he was merely attempting to drive away the harbingers of destruction, to protect a beautiful way of life from ending.

But, after playing with this idea for a while, I still conclude he just had what the Spaniards say is *"mala leche."* That means bad, or sour milk.

They say if, as a baby, your mother suckled you with sour milk then you go through life pissed off about it, with a mean face and sour outlook. That's more likely why he punched me in the face, because all he ever got from his mother's teat was bitter tasting milk.

"Mala leche."

Another working kid, one who actually works with real *"leche"* helping out the *"lechero"* or milkman, is Antonio. He wears the same blue cotton pants, grey shirt, and workingman's uniform as Elias and *"El Carbonero"*.

I meet him later through the guy who becomes my best friend, Manolito. He knows Antonio because they live in the same east of town neighborhood.

Antonio lives in a small house by the side of the girl's orphanage, just outside of town, where his Dad is caretaker. I visit several times at their modest adobe home.

To get there you walk past a dusty playground several hundred feet across where crowds of little orphan girls play behind a high wire fence. They wear identical blue dress uniforms with white collars and, intent on their skip rope and other Spanish kid games, don't seem to look at you as you walk by.

In the small yard off the house Antonio keeps several rabbits in a hutch. One day he proudly shows us how the male rabbit "does it" like a machine gun with the female. Antonio rolls his "r's" like a rapid-fire Sten gun to describe it

"R-r-r-r-r-r-r-rt! Y ....tracatra!"

That last word, *"tracatra"* is a cool local catchall phrase the kids teach me. It means several things, among them: it's a done deal, that's all she wrote, and sexual intercourse.

So you can say:

"Want to learn marbles? Come by. And, *tracatra.*"

Or ... "Their car crashed over the cliff. And, *tracatra.*"

Or ... "He took his girl into the bushes. And, *tracatra.*"

Another thing the local kids teach me is how to steal and eat sugar cane. There are cane fields all over town and to a kid who knows how, they are sort of like candy stores with no one minding the store.

If you've ever had fresh-cut sugar cane you know what I mean.

First, you have to scout a likely field out and walk its perimeters to make sure no one's watching. The one guy you want to make sure isn't around is this local *campesino* hired to protect the fields.

He carries a shotgun loaded with rock salt instead of shot and, if he nails you with it, you're in for a world of searing pain with stinging pellets of rock salt blasted into your backside.

Next, you sneak deep into the field and quickly twist down a likely looking stalk. Then you haul it to the edge of the field and, after making sure the coast is clear, run like hell down the road with it, expecting every second to feel the sting of rock salt pellets biting into your thieving little rear end.

Finally, when you've got your prize safely spirited somewhere safe, it's time for sugar heaven. If you've got a knife, that's good, but the local kids teach me how to peel off the outer stalk with just your teeth.

Once you get to the heart of the cane, you start chewing. Instantly, the most delicious stream of liquid sugar you ever tasted gushes your way. If sugar were heroin, this is the uncut stuff.

To a kid, it's almost like a religious experience.

Eventually, you spit out the dry, useless stalk. You don't actually eat anything with sugar cane, it's more like you drink it. Then you go back for more with your local friends.

As far as teaching these kids baseball, something I had thought I might do, I decide against it. I can't speak very good Spanish yet and only have one mitt.

I also seem to have forgotten to bring my Davy Crockett hat and I don't bring that subject up with my friends. They have no idea who Fess Parker is, or that he played both Davy Crockett and Daniel Boone. Forget it, frontiersmen have no place here in this strange land.

I begin to feel the USA in me begin to slowly drift away and I am helpless to stop it.

Then one day at the ice cream stand, America suddenly calls out to me again from the blue. The stand's tinny radio starts blaring out the Davy Crockett theme song. I get excited.

I hear the banjos launch into the "Born on a mountain top in Tennessee" part so deeply engraved in my heart. Yeah, this is great. Davy and America.

Until they start with the lyrics.

Instead of singing "Davy...Davy Crockett, King of the Wild Frontier," they're singing something else. In Spanish. And it isn't even about Him.

"Pancho....Pancho Lopez, chiquito pero maton."

My heart sinks. I am so far away from America even Davy Crockett has become.....Pancho Lopez.

I feel momentarily as despondent as the great woodsman himself would have been had he found himself marooned on Mars, far from the green forests he knew, and the locals ignored his feats and sang instead about some alien/Spanish guy called....Pancho Lopez.

Rather than bolster my spirits with a stirringly familiar song this wretched "Pancho Lopez" thing only taunts me and underlines how far away I am from America and everything I knew and loved.

I am here thousands of miles away, far from Dad and home, in a land where everything including the language is so unfamiliar even at the ice cream stand they don't have cones, but cut square chunks from a vanilla/chocolate loaf and hand them to you on rectangular wafers making some sort of cold sandwich kind of thing.

As I dig into my melting ice cream sandwich, I also lick my wounds and wonder will when I ever see America again.

But, hey, I'm a kid. At least for the moment, I deal with it and move on. There are things to do, kids to meet. Besides, this is only for a summer. We're going back to America after it's over.

Another Torremolinos kid we meet fairly quickly is Pacquito Flores. His parents own the Flores Hotel right across from the ice cream stand and he likes hanging out with the foreigners, I think in part because he is hoping the *americanas* are interested in a little *tracatra,* like maybe making out or at least a kiss or two.

Pacquito is dark like many an *andaluz* and good looking enough to attract the attention of the ladies.

Early on, when we live in a house whose large garden grounds include a cave by the cliff, a group of us go into the cave one evening with flashlights to watch Pacquito make out with an American girl called Regina.

She's horse crazy and she fancies she's a female horse and he's a Spanish stallion, so after he French kisses her, she stamps her feet and whinnies like a mare in heat. As for Pacquito, he may think the horse part's silly but, like I said, he just fancies a little bit of *tracatra.*

As for me and girls, I'm shy and express disinterest in the opposite sex. But in private, in my own personal inner sanctum, I notice certain ones, though I never say anything about it, who knows why.

Like Sabiliche, a young lady who works at the local hairdressers and goes out with one of the butcher's sons. She's probably sixteen or seventeen, and such a dark haired, Spanish knockout even one of those blind guys who sell lottery tickets on the street would turn his head and exclaim:

"Whoo, boy. Did you see that one!"

Then there are two girls who live in the *Bahondillo* whose names I never know but who make an impact on me nonetheless. One is a chestnut-haired fisherman's daughter I see one day dancing flamenco on a table at a country fiesta.

Torremolinos

There is something about her tan and strong, healthy body and the smooth lines of her jaw and cheeks that compel me to watch her whenever she walks by.

The other is a blonde, presumably store bought blonde, since her eyebrows are black and her skin is dark brown. It's such a sexy combination that golden hair spilling out on brown tanned skin that even a dopey kid like me has to perk up whenever she's near.

These are all, however, older women. By older, I mean like fifteen or sixteen. That makes them unattainable except in a young boy's daydreams.

Nearer my own age, there's the daughter of this older German couple who run the small La Perlilla (that means "little pearl") restaurant. Her mom makes the most scrumptious German *apfel cooken* or apple pie. We look forward to it whenever we eat there.

And the daughter, I kind of fancy her. She runs with the village kids; she grew up in Torremolinos. She's tall and strong and tanned, and talks to you in that direct sort of in your face, almost confrontational way German girls do.

I see her at the beach with their huge speckled great Dane and begin talking to her now and then, especially after her dog knocks me down one day. Maybe that's a sign, fido picked me out for his little German mistress.

But, if something is going to develop, it never has time to happen.

An American Jewish guy, a World War II survivor originally from Germany, comes to town on vacation and goes to enjoy a nice Deutschland meal at the La Perlilla. He takes one look at Willy, the owner of the place and my prospective girlfriend's dad, and nearly has a fit.

He recognizes Willy as one of the brutal Nazi guard's at his concentration camp, he's named Helmut not Willy.

That night, the Jewish guy gets stinking drunk at the Bar Central, tells the whole town about Willy's war criminal past and, fortified by Spanish brandy, threatens to get a gun and shoot the ex-Nazi dead on the spot. Swears that he will do it tomorrow.

The next day the La Perlilla is closed. Willy, his wife, and my little German crush are gone forever, vanished like the Little Pearl restaurant in the night.

Love just isn't for me yet, not even when its handed to me on a platter.

When we live by the church there is, you see, a village girl my age, who I am quietly informed by local kids, fancies me.

Unfortunately, I do not fancy her. She's slightly chubby and has curly brunette hair and, while her face is cute enough, she giggles extremely loudly whenever I exit the house and stares coyly in my direction.

This embarrasses me so mortally I take to sneaking out of the house the back way, over a wall, down a storm drain and through a dark alleyway.

Anything to not hear her annoying giggle.

That's how it is at this time in Torremolinos and maybe how it is almost always for most everyone.

The ones who want you, you want to run away from. And you never find your way to get near the ones you'd really like to take out for an evening stroll.

And *tracatra*.

Torremolinos

David M. Johnson

3
Titi

IT'S A STEAMY HOT MID MORNING IN TORREMOLINOS and people bustle about their errands at the top of the *Calle San Miguel* where it ends at the main *carretera*, the highway leading up and down the coast.

There's enough traffic at this hour Saturday to require a white-coated traffic *policía*, alternately stopping the highway traffic, then starting it with a sharp whistle and a sweeping gesture of his white gloved hands.

Ladies carrying straw bags with the day's shopping stroll from the market further up the hill and head home with fresh produce and meat and fish taken the night before from the Mediterranean.

A mule-driven cart carries red bricks down the highway towards the *Carihuela*, the cart driver hurrying his animal on with a clucking of his tongue and the rolling "r's" cry of *"ar-r-r-r-r-rrre, muuuuula!"* or even: *"Sooooo bor-rr-rr-riccooooo!"*

The beast's hooves momentarily slip on the grey cobblestones as he strains at his load and picks up the pace as a few cars and a groaning, overloaded bus pass it by. Underneath the brick laden cart trots a scruffy Andaluz dog, held by a leash tied to the wooden axle.

With a sharp whistle and a histrionic gesture the *policía* halts all the highway traffic and holds his hands out to hold the vehicles steady.

He glances up the road towards the road leading to the market and the hillside village or *Calvario* above it.

Obviously some very important vehicle must be about to approach.

But instead of the rumble of a big truck or bus, or even the popping sewing machine buzz of a cheap red *Guzzi* moto, you hear a man's high voice making this strange sort of rhythmic sound:

"Uh-uht! Uh-uht! Uh-uht!"

Then the man pulls into view and the villagers smile at a familiar sight.

It's just Titi, driving through on his motorcycle, an everyday common sight that's unusual only for one instantly obvious reason.

Titi doesn't actually have a motorcycle.

Instead, he holds his hands out in the air as if he were grasping the handlebars of some powerful machine. And he hops along at a pretty good clip, somehow managing to spring forward quite a distance with each hop even though he always lands with both feet together and takes off much the same way.

The overall effect is sort of like a human pogo stick as he descends the road from the *Mercado*, deftly manages the turn into the *Plaza Central* and then he hangs a left down *Calle San Miguel*.

As he "drives" by, you get a glimpse of a grinning man, about thirty or so, with thin gaunt features, impossibly huge ears, crooked front teeth and high cheekbones, leathery sort of skin and clear blue eyes that look to somewhere so far off you can't even begin to imagine.

Then he is past you and headed down the *Calle*, still grasping the handlebars of his imaginary *moto*, his cry echoing back.

"Uh-uht! Uh-uht! Uh-Uht!"

With a flourish of his hands, the *policía* allows the traffic to resume and life bustles on as usual. The fact that a fully-grown man without a motorcycle just pretended to ride one through town is barely even noticed by the morning shoppers or the waiting highway traffic.

Asi es la vida.

That was the way things are in Torremolinos when it comes to people who are a trifle odd. They aren't put away or secluded, they are just part of the daily tapestry of life. And Titi is just one of them, the one with the motorcycle no one else can see.

Another time, we are told, the cop actually stops Titi and writes him a ticket. Thunderstruck and surprised (and likely not too literate) Titi shows the ticket to a tourist friend who assures him it's okay, there won't be any monetary fine, it's only a warning ticket.

Apparently the *policía* spotted something wrong with Titi's motorcycle: the headlamp is too dim.

The first time we meet Titi is when we arrive on the bus from Algeciras and the bus driver pulls all our luggage out. Immediately, this tall, gaunt stranger seizes our suitcases and hoarsely screams out a weird cry, sort of a strangled "ahhhh-ahhhhh-ah!" like he was being choked to death, with a big happy grin on his face.

Alarmed, my mother seizes the other side of the suitcase handles to stop this odd, wheezing stranger from stealing all our earthly belongings. They are having a sort of tug of war until someone who speaks English explains to her.

"This man...he is Titi. He carry suitcases for *pesetas*. *Pesetas* for Titi and Titi's mother. He no can speak. Just make sounds. Titi want to make some *pesetas*."

That settled, my mother agrees.

Titi happily escorts us and carries our suitcases south down the *carretera* to a hotel, beaming and wheezing all the while as we kids uneasily try to keep as far away as possible from what we consider a real nut job.

Had we known that he actually rode a non-existent motorcycle we would have been doubly apprehensive.

But after living in the town awhile we get used to him. Hey, he is part of it, always has been. We're the strange ones here, *los extranjeros*, a word that indicates "foreigners" but literally translates as "strangers." And we're delighted to see Titi ride through town.

It all works out pretty well, except for the time Titi carefully parks his imaginary motorcycle just outside the *Bar Quitapenas* (or "PainKiller" Bar) and goes off about some business. Soon, some unwitting *turista* parks his car right in the same spot where Titi left his precious motorcycle.

When the *turista* returns to his car he's met with a loud wheezing harangue from Titi who is obviously pissed about something. A crowd begins to gather.

Baffled and highly confused, the car driver is finally enlightened by a fairly tippled English man emerging from the bar who tells him:

"Look, mate. It's simple. You've parked your bloody car right on top of Titi's motorcycle."

The watching crowd nods and murmurs in assent as the Englishman weaves off, several sheets to the wind.

Alarmed that he might have indeed done such a careless thing, the motorist gets down on his knees and looks carefully under the car to see what sort of damage he's done to the broken motorcycle.

Finding nothing, he stands up looking more surprised than before, looks around wide-eyed at the crowd of smiling, nodding people, and quickly gets in and drives off, probably convinced the whole village is populated by lunatics.

It isn't, of course. But the local habit of keeping around and out in the open those who might elsewhere be deemed a little off is new to me. And, on occasion, frightening.

Consider, for instance, Crazy Man.

If you walk down *Calle San Miguel*, past the small shops at the top, it becomes residential and you find yourself strolling by whitewashed walls and the open doors of people's homes.

Suddenly a man springs out at you from a doorway, crouched on all fours, growling low like a dog and snarling nonsense syllables.

"Abala abala abalalablab!!!!!"".

Springing back you see a madly grinning man of about thirty or forty, pale blue eyes far apart, half lidded and demented, face clean-shaven but with a blue five o'clock shadow, babbling and gesticulating and growling at you while sitting on his haunches, all the while holding and drooling copiously on a red rubber ball.

"That's Crazy Man," my friend David Stahl tells me the first time this wild creature leaps out at me from his doorway.

"They keep him chained in there. A big, strong chain around his waist. That's so he can't come all the way out and get you. Which, believe me, you wouldn't want to happen," he explains.

"One kid in the town walked too close and Crazy Man got him and dragged him inside. He was never seen again and no one dared go in after him."

I didn't entirely believe that. In fact, my mother tells us Crazy Man is just severely retarded, but his family loves him so much they keep him there at home with them.

That makes more sense to me but still, whenever I walk down that stretch of *San Miguel*, I give Crazy Man's door a wide berth. This way, in case he needs one more kid dragged into his lair and finished off, it isn't going to be me.

On a friendlier note, there's Donkey Binky. That is the name of a cart donkey as well as the name we call its owner. He's the village *carbonero*, or coal merchant. And my mother tells us that there's something just a little "off" about Donkey Binky.

The man, not the donkey.

As a kid I can't say I really notice it although he laughs a lot when there don't seem to be any jokes, and has that same far-off look in his eyes Titi does. But we love him because he lets us ride with him in his donkey cart full of coal.

We clippety-clop from house to house to deliver whatever chunks of *carbon* people need for heating and cooking, which is plenty. At this time in Torremolinos lots of the houses don't have any heating other than from coal heaters, and most cooking is done on coal-fired iron stoves.

Every morning our maid has to start a wood fire in the stove, and put coal on top and wave at it with a handmade straw fan to get it going before she can add more coal and cook us up any *huevos fritos*. I help her fan the fire until the oil in the frying pan gets hot enough. She tells me when it's good and ready."

"*Cuándo el aceite echa humo.*"

"When the oil sends out smoke."

Then you crack the eggs and drop them in. And you use the spatula to splash the smoking hot oil on top of the eggs to fry them crisp all over, top as well as bottom.

Very tasty, especially with churros. *Muy sabroso!*

Not only do they not fry eggs the same way here, a lot of the food is way different from anything we knew back home.

Like the first time we see a plate of *calamares* or fried squid, including the squiggly little legs, we are not too sure about the idea. Back in America nobody eats squid in 1957. But after a few tentative tastes we quickly get aboard and even the slippery tentacles go sliding down our hungry little gullets.

Same with *chanquetes* heaps of battered and deep fried minnows, totally intact with their little eyes peering out at you through the layer of crisp fried batter. Are you really going to eat those whole little fish, brains and guts and all? One timid taste is all it takes. Yes sir, we love them *chanquetes* and grab them by the handful.

Another guaranteed kid pleaser is called *coquinas,* and it's tiny baby clams, not much bigger than medium olives. These are cooked in their shells in a pan with olive oil, garlic and a little white wine and parsley. Then you grab them and slurp them right up from their shells. Yum.

We have the same enthusiasm for *tortilla española,* a round cake-like omelet made with potatoes and onions. Yum.

Then, of course, there's paella, perhaps the king of Spanish dishes, all the tastier when cooked outdoors over an open fire in a large flat pan with two handles. Heaps of short-grain rice colored yellow by savory saffron enveloping tender chicken pieces and sausage and swimming with squid, shrimp, mussels and clams, a bulls eye to a seafood loving little kid like me.

Yes, food isn't the same here in Torremolinos as it was in Bethesda. We may now and then miss hamburgers, Chinese and Italian food at restaurants Dad took us to, massive ice cream Sundaes at Giffords, and summer night frozen treats from the magical frosty freezer in the Good Humour truck. Now and then we get nostalgic for them.

But what they are replaced by is by no means a step down. Just a step to the side, and a delicious one at that. Every evening as the maid fans the coal in the stove till it glows red hot, we watch in wonder to see what she will make for *la cena.*

That's why Donkey Binky hauls that cart of coal around the town: that's the fuel you cook with. Forget electric heating units or gas –fired stoves.

Coal, baby, coal.

Another cart with yet another donkey travels around town carrying huge rectangular blocks of ice insulated by straw. The driver cuts off the size chunk that fits in what passes in your house as the refrigerator. Then he uses a large pincher tool to lift the ice chunk and carry it in to your cooling box.

Our food doesn't stay cool thanks to electricity. It's in a true, old-fashioned "icebox", as in an airtight box cooled by an actual chunk of ice slowly melting in a compartment in the top.

We have clearly travelled way back in time here. All the way to ice cooled fridges and stoves that run on coal. You might almost expect to see steam-driven cars. Nothing seems or looks the same as it did back home.

To a kid fresh from America, this place is stranger and stranger.

Even the music is weird. Back in the States, friend's older sisters were totally in love with this guy called Elvis and the radio played his music and other calmer American stuff by people like Perry Como and Dean Martin.

Driving around with his Chevy radio on, our Dad always turns it up when "Singing the Blues" comes on by a singer called Guy Mitchell.

"That's what some people call hillbilly music, " Dad says back then. "But I kind of like it."

By contrast in Spain you hear a lot of this rhythmic South American/ Caribbean kind of songs with lots of drums and percussion. One tune that strikes me is called *"Esperanza"* about a lady of that name who apparently can only dance the cha-cha-cha.

"Esperanza, Esperanza, solo sabes bailar el cha-cha-cha."

I gather over repeated listening that the singer's lament isn't so much that she only knows this one dance but that she's always dancing it with other guys.

Got to watch these Spanish women.

Another song I like shows off the Spaniards ability to make fun of almost anything, including sometimes themselves. At the time in Africa the Belgian Congo is going through a bloody upheaval, with the province of Katanga in flames and the leader Patrice Lumumba assassinated. The Spanish find in this mayhem something funny enough to create a humorous song about it. On top of a rhythmic bed of singers repeating *"Lumumba, Katanga! Lumumba, Katanga!..."* the lead singers shout: *"Que pasa en El Congo?"* (What's going on in The Congo?)

The apparently side-splitting reply is *"Que al Blanco que cogen le hacen mondongo!"* (Any White they catch they cook into a stew!).

Who can explain humor? I like the rhythm part anyway. It's catchy.

In Torremolinos there are also here many door-to-door peddlers, something we never saw back in Chevy Chase.

We get daily visits from a guy they call "Pedro, The Egg Man. " That's what he sells, eggs.

Jokingly they say Pedro is *"El hombre con los huevos."* "The man with the eggs." The joke here is *huevos* also means "balls" as in *"cojones"* so it also means he's "The Man with the Balls.

Maybe Pedro has too many *huevos* for his own good. I am told the maid's are really disgusted by him because he says "things" to them. I don't understand what that means. But years later when I picture him in my memory's eye, I see this middle-aged fat guy with a white cap leering at the maids and he does look kind of pervy.

In the right season, peddlers also come by selling fresh strawberries, honey, peaches, asparagus, and there's a man who comes with cheeses like *manchego* and *cabrales*.

Plus, there's the knife sharpener. He rides around on his bicycle blowing these super high notes on this small whistle to let you know here's there. Then he sets his bike upside down on its seat, pumps the pedals and they rapidly spin a grindstone. When he sharpens your knives on this, it sends out a shower of sparks that are mesmerizing and almost magical to a little kid.

Afterwards the maids have sharper blades to cut and prepare whatever they are cooking on those coal stoves.

And the heat that makes all that cooking happen comes from the bags of coal we tourist kids help the *carbonero* deliver in his cart.

When Mr. Donkey Binky and his little apprentices (that's us) arrive at a home that needs coal, he looks at us and laughs like something really funny has happened. Then he carries the irregular chunks of coal inside, nestled in large straw sacks with handles that he slings over his back.

Then it's back to the cart and his cry that starts the donkey up, and gives him his nickname: "Donkey Binky! Arrrrrreee!"

There are also here and there people wearing dark glasses standing around the street, screaming very loudly, which startles me a at first. But I find out that this is their job, screaming out: *"veinte iguales para hoy."*

What that means is they are selling 20, or *veinte,* identical looking lottery tickets called *iguales,* which means "equals" or " the same".

And *"para hoy"* means for today.

I learn these are blind people gainfully employed in this fashion, selling *iguales.* It's sort of a charity disguised as employment: they're not begging, they're hawking tickets with their loud cry of *"Veinte iguales para hoy!".*

There is even a local joke my Spanish friends tell me that one of these blind lottery vendors gets on a bus. And then he cuts a deadly fart. Then he farts big time again. So one of the passengers then throws him out the bus window.

The other passengers cry out "Why did you throw that poor blind man out the window!?" He calmly explains "Because he was yelling out: *veinte iguales para hoy."*

Or: "twenty of the same for today".

Another, darker oddity we see around Torremolinos, and even more when our mother takes us to the big market in Málaga, are people maimed in the Spanish Civil War. There are a lot of guys missing various limbs who hobble around on crutches or whatever.

I have never seen sights like that in the scrubbed clean happy suburbs of Chevy Chase.

But, here, with the war less than twenty years old, it's everywhere and out in the open. It's the kind of stuff that makes a kid like me stare and wonder, "How did that happen?"

Maybe it's so visible because the Spaniards don't try to hide ugly things. Or because the Civil War they had was so particularly vicious.

From 1934 to 1939 half a million Spaniards die, in five brutal years that are even bloodier than America's own Civil War. We're talking about a war of mind-boggling viciousness and horror.

During the war years things get rough around Málaga, the Andalusian province Torremolinos is in. In the beginning of the war, the province throws its lot in with the left, the anarchists, socialists, communists and etc.

Malagueños torch churches and execute over 2,500 priests and suspected nationalists. The different factions also spend so much time arguing with each other and engaging in power fights that they never put a coherent defense plan together.

In 1937 payback time arrives as Franco and his allies close in. After heavy bombardment of Malaga from ships off shore and from Franco's bomber aircraft, nationalist and Italian troops tighten a noose around the city. The population that can flees up the one narrow coast road towards Almeria, hounded by tanks and planes dropping bombs and strafing the terrified civilians, as well as shelling from ships off the coast.

Overhead, trying vainly to protect the fleeing hordes, are the tattered remnants of French writer Andre Malraux's volunteer squadron of Potez 54 aircraft. Out of gas, out of parts, they give what resistance they can against Franco's modern fleet of German and Italian airplanes. Malraux is wounded twice attempting to defend Madrid in this same manner.

This dangerous retreat up the coast by a terrified and beset upon fleeing populace is referred to in history books as the "Malaga-Almeria road massacre."

Those who stayed behind aren't so lucky either. Close to 7,000 are executed on the beautiful beaches where tourists cavort today or against the walls of the bombed out buildings.

For most of the surviving Malagueños times are tough after the war, they have to struggle just to get by. One of the maids we have, Lola, brings this home to me one day when she tells me, that back when she was a little girl and they were all starving during the war, one day her father managed to catch and kill a stray cat.

They had such a feast with the roast cat they held a big happy party the whole family still remembers, dancing and singing.

Now, in 1957, I see hobbling around the streets of Malaga some of those who lived through this brutal time. In this very strange land we find ourselves everything seems to be out in the open, including life's abnormalities, whether the cruel war victims or the more charming aberrations like Titi and Donkey Binky and Crazy Man.

It is unsettling at first that everything is so different. The food, the clothes, the music and then seeing some of the odder people who walk around in Torremolinos, people who probably in America would have been kept apart from the rest of us, maybe even institutionalized, but it is also pretty cool they are just part of everyday life.

They make it richer. I know that now when I picture Titi ecstatically riding his imaginary motorcycle down San Miguel coming the other way, past Crazy Man's house, is the coal man's cart with my friend Dana Ericson standing in front wearing the carbonero's beret.

Tugging on the clip-clopping donkey's reins, the little American boy happily cries out:

"Donnnnnkey Binnnky! Arrrrrreee!!!"

Torremolinos

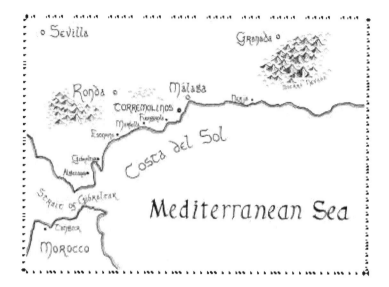

4
Torremolinos 1957

SO WHERE EXACTLY DO WE NOW FIND OURSELVES and what does it look like?

Maybe it's time I took you by the hand and we made a little tour of Torremolinos. (By the way, you should pronounce it as "Toe-ray-moe-leen-ohs." Or just "Torre" for short)

Back then Torremolinos is two parts fishing village, one part mountain village and, in the summer in particular, a rapidly growing part that is just beginning to be a resort. That's the part that will soon swallow the others, chew them up and spit them out on the altar of big tourist money *turismo*.

But that's the future. You and I are back in 1957.

Picture a rugged range of small semi-arid mountains, rocky and brown, dotted with scrubby and often fragrant rosemary bushes and a few dry, scraggly trees. The peaks rise maybe three or four thousand feet high, into a sunny blue sky.

Then the hills slope down for three miles to meet several hundred yards of yellow/white sand beach that extend lazily to the lapping waves of the sky blue Mediterranean. All the way west almost to the rock of Gibraltar this beach stretch is dubbed *La Costa Del Sol*, the Sun Coast.

To the east of Torremolinos, the beach extends all the way to the city of Málaga about 11 miles or 18 kilometers away. The *Costa* extends further east past Velez-Málaga to beyond Nerja and its prehistoric caves with their Paleolithic wall paintings.

To the immediate west of Torremolinos, the beach is broken by a jagged volcanic cliff 200 feet high with rocks so sharp they can cut your bare feet.

On the western side of this cliff lies the large and poor fishing village of *La Carihuela.* If you dare swim the quarter mile around the cliffs (and I learn to) you can get there easily.

"Hidropedal" rounding cliff towards Carihuela fishing village

Up above the beaches that stretch away on the eastern side of this cliff, sitting proudly up on the plateau like a castle on the hill, complete with it's own watchtower, is the center of the town called Torremolinos.

That's where the *carretera* or highway that runs up and down the coast cuts through town. (Don't get me wrong when I say highway, it is just a paved two-lane road, nothing like what we called highway in the U.S. even back then, and don't go thinking the paving is that good either).

Just in from the beaches down below either side of the cliff are the two fishing villages that are part of Torremolinos. On the eastern or Málaga side of the cliffs, the *Bahondillo*, and further west in the direction of Gibraltar is the bigger and poorer *Carihuela*. On the sands in front of these villages are the wooden, painted fishing boats with their triangular sails, much like Arab dhows.

Sleepy main street of Bahondillo fishing village

Above the plateau part, stretching maybe a half-mile up the gentler part of the mountain slope is *El Calvario*, the mountain part of the village named for the Calvary hill in Jerusalem where Christ was crucified by the Romans.

There isn't much up in *El Calvario* beyond simple whitewashed houses lining either side of the bumpy dirt road that leads up through it towards the mountains.

It's hotter up in the *El Calvario* because it's further away from the Mediterranean and its cooling sea breezes. Consequently, when we first get there, very few foreigners live up there, it's mostly locals and fairly poor ones at that.

As we take our little walking tour up through this higher village, we can see the village people through the opened doors of their one or two-room home's doors, widowed ladies in black, kids in shorts, toddlers in their T-shirts and otherwise naked, guys wearing berets or those Spanish village guy caps, saddling up their burros to go about some mountain business or other.

Walk with me in the fierce summer heat far enough up to where the dirt road runs out of houses but keeps going anyway. About a quarter mile later where it ends, on the right we see a large red and yellow stucco building that looks kind of institutional.

That's *El Reformatorio*, the reformatory, a place for juvenile delinquents. Sometimes you see them outside playing soccer in their blue uniforms with their shaved heads, but usually they're inside doing whatever Spanish j.d.'s have to do when they're being reformed.

You rarely see the reformatory kids around the village except on holy days when their bugle and drum band marches in the processions through town. I am kind of scared of them because they are all supposed to be "bad kids" and they have these real marine recruit type shaved haircuts.

But I also admire the precision and serious discipline of their little band in its blue shorts and blue shirts when they come to play and march on village *fiesta* days. They play some mean *Semana Santa* tunes, marching in step as the village men slowly carry and sway a flower-bedecked float with the crying *Virgen.*

Usually, the processions are led by local officials, the mayor and others who matter, as well as high church officials and military figures. Behind them, the nuns from the orphanage, led by their head prioress.

Next march the *guardia civiles,* the local military cops. They are stern-looking in their dull green uniforms with leather straps across the fronts, tri-cornered black hats from the era of Napoleon, and shoulder carried machine guns.

In the much grander Holy week processions in Málaga, there are also hordes of people dressed like Klu Klux Klansmen in America, with scary peaked white hoods with eyeholes. We are told this has nothing to do with the KKK and burning crosses, just with Jesus and his whole deal. Still, in Malaga they look spooky. I don't actually remember any real hooded dudes in Torremolinos.

Next in our village march the reformatory kids swaying to an almost hypnotic and solemn deep drum beat:

Brum! Brum! Brum! Da-Dum! Brum! Brum! Brum! Da-Dum!

Behind them, the village men carrying the statue of the Virgen sway slowly back and forth to the steady beat. The Virgen seems to shake as each slow step lands, sculptured tears coursing down her sad, mournful cheeks, decorative flowers shaking with each coordinated step.

Every so often, the reformatory band lifts its bugles in exact precision and blows a serious refrain about suffering and the cross.

Ba-da-<u>dah</u>! Bah-da-<u>dah</u>! Dat-datdatdat- datdat-datdat dah <u>dah</u>-dahhh!

The whole effect is trancelike and dead serious, to a little American kid even scary.

This is a far cry from the happy Fourth of July parades down Wisconsin Avenue back in Bethesda, with high school bands, horn-blowing fire trucks, clowns throwing candy and those lovely cheerleaders marching in step with their white boots, pom-poms, perfect young knees and ecstatic white toothed smiles.

No. Here in Torremolinos this parade, like the local religion is about solemnity, suffering and sorrow.

There is no happy here, no clowns throwing candy, no white-booted cheerleaders with pom-poms. Just the shaven-headed boys from the reformatory drumming out the way life goes down out here, including the suffering of Christ and all the tortured and bloodied saints, in this strange new land.

Those tough kids from the reformatory, locked in step to the beat of their drummers, raise their bugles and blow away about Christ and the cross and the whole Catholic deal. They really lay it down like they mean it.

I hope today that as many of them as possible came out of that mountain reformatory and have had good lives. I have no idea whether that's true or not, it's just how I feel remembering them.

But back to our tour. Coming down the dirt road from the *Calvario*, just above the main town, we find the town market, a circular white washed building with a green roof, built around an open central courtyard. Every morning except Sunday it bustles with farmers, fishermen and other merchants selling their wares to the local people and to the foreigners or their *chicas*, the maids sent to do the morning's shopping with straw baskets to carry it off in.

We stroll down from the market a few hundred yards and the now paved road descends to the Plaza Central, the main square where the coastal highway goes through town.

Center of Torremolinos, the Plaza Central and main coastal highway

There is a small island of a park with some tall trees in the center of the square, and a *gasolinera* where cars and motorcycles fill up with petrol from two small red hand-cranked gas pumps with glass cylinders that alternately fill and empty with foamy gasoline as it gets pumped.

On the southern side of the square is a cafe with lots of open-air tables out front. This is the Bar Central, the social center of town at the time, the place the adults, locals and foreigners alike, gather in the evening for a glass of wine or *amontillado* while sitting outside at a table watching the passing parade of life in Torremolinos.

As a kid, I like when our mother takes us to the Bar Central and we order a steaming *cafe con leche*, sugaring it up with several large cubes of *azucar*, always taking the sugar cube out of its paper wrapper and just dipping one end into the coffee so you watch the tan liquid get drawn upwards into the sugar cube as if by some magical and immutable force of nature.

Bar Central. A social hub to many. But no hamburgers to us.

We sip the sugary *café con leche* and have to admit Spain has a few pretty good things. But even with these sweet coffees, we kids quickly agree with each other it really can't match up to places back home, because The Bar Central lacks the one essential thing that makes America the great nation it is today..

Hamburgers.

Hey, Spaniards, where are the hamburgers?

"Hey, Waiter, do you have any hamburgers...you know,um....hamburguesas?"

"No, señorito, aquí en El Bar Central no tenemos hamburguesas."

Then this place stinks.

You see, *café con leche* is all very fine and dandy, but if you ain't got hamburgers, you ain't got nothing, at least to us.

No *hamburguesas*, no *nada*.

Towards the western end of the square in the morning there is a *churreria* that sells doughy hot *churros* all tied up together in a green river reed and wrapped in newspaper. When it's your turn to get them you carry them back down *Calle San Miguel*, the warm package in your one arm, the other occupied feeding a hot *churro* into your hungry little face.

In the evening there's an open-air *marisquería* instead of the *churreria*, with white-aproned guys who shuck fat iced clams for you and squirt fresh *limon* on them.

Heaven to a seafood lover like me.

In between there and the Bar Central, on the north side of the Plaza Central, there's a two-story yellow stone building that houses the Banco Vizcaya.

In front of that bank is a large stone fountain with pools where the water spills out where the local donkeys and horses can drink. Two brass spigots on either side that emit a constant flow of cool fresh water straight from a spring high in the mountains above the village.

Take a drink from that fountain and you have never tasted water that is as refreshing and gloriously soul-satisfying as the cool liquid from the spigots.

You lean over to drink it, or cup your hands to catch it and then in the heat of day greedily drink it in, the water from that long since gone *fuente*. The fresh mountain spring water has a subtle taste and smooth almost thickness I can't find words to fully describe the taste. Let's just say sipping Evian is like drinking mud puddle water next to it.

Left, the town fountain. Large building ahead, El Mañana night club.

Now we head towards the sea down the *Calle San Miguel,* which will eventually lead us straight all the way to the cliff that stands several hundred feet up about a quarter mile from the sea.

First, at the top of *San Miguel,* we find a few restaurants with tables out front on the narrow pebble paved sidewalks. And a couple of pastry shops with fancy-looking Spanish meringues and cakes that somehow never taste even a fraction as good as they look, a few small Spanish mom and pop grocery stores, one of the town's two butcher shops, and a few doors leading to people's homes.

And a cobblers/shoeshine place.

As you head down San Miguel towards the sea, behind the houses on your right you can discover a narrow alleyway with fresh water from the mountains, destined for irrigation. The water courses noisily down a cement channel in it's middle. At one point, this channel is parted to create a long pool where local women wash their family clothes and pound them dry and clean on slanted corrugated cement ramps.

This resembles in no fashion how your Mom used to take out the Tide back in Chevy Chase and load up the electric washing machine. It's more like those photos you see in National Geographic where Afghan women pound clothes clean on river stones.

But that's how it goes here.

Back on San Miguel a few hundred meters down, we find the line of white washed houses is broken by the train tracks that lead east to Málaga, west to Fuengirola and Marbella. Just down the track in the latter direction is the small stucco and red brick railroad station where the puffing steam engine pulls in several times a day.

Just after the tracks, as we head on towards the sea, there is the Bar Quitapenas, a big noontime drinking place and home of a local guy I hear my mother refer to as the "town drunk."

When you consider all the drinking that is going on, thanks to the rich foreigners, the notion of just one town drunk is actually pretty ludicrous.

Across from the Quitapenas is a *panadería*, or bakery, where you can buy all manner of fresh breads and rolls as long as you're not looking for plastic-wrapped, pre-sliced Wonder Bread.

And don't go looking for Hostess Twinkies or Ring Dings or even English muffins, mí amigo.

Calle San Miguel. Right, Bar Quitapenas ("Painkiller" Bar)

They also sell a local delicacy called *tortas*, cinnamon brown sort of sweet rolls, caked with granular sugar and wrapped in an oily paper. They are flavored with some local spices and made all the more delicious by these aromatic mountain bushes thrown onto the fire when they bake.

Periodically, little donkeys clip clop up and wait outside the white washed walls of the bakery loaded up with tied bundles of these fragrant bushes and their intoxicating smell drifts down the *calle* for you to sniff and imagine biting into a fresh *torta.*

Heading further down *San Miguel*, there are just a few stores. Another *almacén*, or local grocery storefront, and a *ferretería* or hardware store, but don't go thinking Ace Hardware or the like. No aisles, just a counter you order at and stuff hanging up on the sides and above.

Further on there is a small lumberyard just next to another fountain of mountain spring water. You can walk into the lumberyard and watch them cut stuff. And there is a scraps pile you can scavenge free things from to build whatever projects you can come up with.

After the lumberyard the *calle* opens up momentarily into an informal wide sort of plaza just before hanging a short right uphill to the town church. It is all homes and no stores, unless you count two little old ladies in black who sell chewing gum, candies and cigarettes from inside their one room home.

Whenever we part the curtain that serves as their door and venture in there, clutching a peseta or two to buy huge jawbreakers, the black clad ladies smile and laugh at each other and refer to us as *"angelitos,"* little angels.

They are so sweet and warm, if there actually are any angels, I bet that's who they're hanging with now.

Now we're at the town church, a fairly large, yet simple whitewashed structure, covered with red brick tiles on the roof and lined with small red bricks on its twin bell towers.

Whenever the townspeople walk by the front of the church, we notice they make the sign of the cross on themselves, either out of respect for the church or maybe, we reason, to ward off evil things like vampires. Their right hands touch their foreheads, then touch their chest over the heart, then the other side, then their stomach and back up to be kissed by the lips.

"That's so their lips can lick off the dirt that is on their clothes and has stuck to their Catholic fingers," my brother Mark tells us.

We're not so sure.

Sometimes, Mark, Mimi and I sneak into the church during services and watch from the darker corners. It's very ornate inside and full of statues of saints, some them dying gruesome and painful deaths, which seems to be part of the appeal of this religion. Not a big come-on to us, the tortuous slow death thing, but somebody digs it.

As the priest deeply sings words in Latin, a dead language nobody in the church or town apparently understands, a choirboy comes down the aisle swinging a golden pot that spews smoke from the burning incense inside it. We have to admit it's a pretty spooky show, but have no idea what it's about.

From Unitarian Sunday school in Bethesda, we've heard a lot about Jesus and some of the Bible stories, but this is Torremolinos: with the Latin and the smoke and the suffering dying statues, this is something else. In America, Jesus seemed to be about love and good things and happy.

Here, not so much the happy stuff.

Directly behind the church, a small alleyway runs between a row of simple houses and behind these on a promontory over the cliff is the town's namesake: a crumbling old watchtower, at one time a mill. Hence the town's name "Torremolinos": tower- mill, *torre- molino.*

The tower is semi-crumbling and the door is locked so you can't climb it. But you get an amazing view leaning on the green painted iron railing in front of it that keeps you from tumbling several hundred feet down the cliff. Right below us, spread out in a sea of white wash and red brick roofs are the hundred or so houses of the *Bahondillo*, still at this point somewhat of a fishing village but with summer houses interspersed here and there.

Look further out and beyond the fishing village you see some fields of waving sugar cane and corn that give way to the yellow sands of the beach, dotted with a few straw huts, some primitive beach cabanas and painted wooden fishing boats, their triangular sails furled.

Now look off to your left, you can see more farmland as far as the eye can see, and a narrow strip of beach that stretches off and curves out where the *Rio Guadiana* meets the sky blue sea.

Beyond that, in the distance the city of Málaga and high above it, the brown *Sierra Moreno* mountains.

On a crystal clear day, above and beyond them to the right, you spot the snow-capped *Sierra Nevada's* that loom above Granada on the other side. People can ski the *Sierra Nevadas* in the morning, get in a car and sun themselves on the *Costa Del Sol* beaches that afternoon.

Unobstructed view to Málaga from overlook. We lived in lower left house.

Now, let's leave the view from the railing and walk down the cobblestone and cement steps that wind down the cliff into the Bahondillo. We walk through the dirt roads of the fishing village, go another few hundred yards past fields of corn and sugar cane with the sea breeze sighing through them, and we're at the Mediterranean.

Gentle waves lap the sand; the Mediterranean sea rarely has big ones except when storms are nearby. A few crude bamboo and river reed cabanas rustle in the wind and the aroma of fresh grilled fish wafts over from the whitewashed beach restaurants further west where the cemetery road winds down to the sands.

Walk further on, and the rocky cliff blocks our way, jutting defiantly right out into the sea.

Carihuela fishing village beach. Beyond the cliff Torremolinos beach.

If you care to swim around the cliff, or take the long hot way over it and down the *carretera*, we wind up at the *Carihuela*, the other fishing village. This one, unlike the *Bahondillo*, is set right on the shore. It's bigger and poorer than its cousin village.

Heading further west, we see a few one or two-story hotels, some modest summer homes for rich Spaniards from the cities and, after that, just more farmland and beaches so empty you can usually have them to yourself.

This is the little world we've been told we will spend our summer in, one that in many respects hasn't changed in centuries. It's so unlike the modern bustle of Washington, D.C., and the America of Mickey Mouse and Superman on television and super highways and supermarkets and hamburgers and Wonder Bread and Twinkies, we might just as well be on the surface of another planet.

Unfortunately this planet, or at least the simple village way of life we see before us, is about as ill-fated as if it was named Krypton and this is its final days with no super hero or hardy frontiersman coming to save it.

You and I have just taken a tour of a doomed world.

5
Los extranjeros

IT'S THE TALK OF THE TOWN, all over Torremolinos.

Mrs. Cooke has really outdone herself this time. And she has done it in one of the very cradles of bullfighting, the 300-year-old venerated *plaza de toros* of the nearby mountain town of Ronda, in the middle of an actual ongoing bullfight.

It seems the *toreros* were flagging just a bit, not really pressing the issue with the bull with enough *cojones*, or at least not in Bobbie Cooke's opinion.

So fuming there in her expensive ringside seat she figures it's about time someone showed them how it was properly done.

She jumps down into the *callejon*, the protected inner alley where the toreros can retreat to be safe from the bull. Then, before the surprised toreros can act, she slips through the *burladero*, the narrow passageway to the ring, and steps onto the blazing sands of the arena.

Apparently both bullfighters and a full-grown fighting bull alike are so shocked they stand motionless and just gawk open-mouthed at the absolutely unexpected apparition: a curvaceous *americana* blonde in her 30's, wearing tight yellow toreador pants, sandals, a silk blouse and movie-star type sunglasses, suddenly standing in the ring.

Unchallenged, at least for the moment, Bobbie stands on the golden sands of the arena and launches into her version of the *faena,* the final act of a corrida.

Bobbie seems to think what is needed to get this party going is some version of the Lindy.

So she dances it wildly for the 6,000 spectators, 30 or so toreros and one 800 lb. bull that's beginning to eye her as if this dance might be reason enough to charge, goaded even further by Bobbie's taunting shouts.

"Toro! Toro! Ah-hey, Torooo!!!"

Fortunately, before the bull charges, the bullfighters recover their senses and hustle her out of harm's way into the uniformed arms of the local *guardia*, who promptly lock her in *la carcel.*

When her husband weaves his way there from the *plaza de toros* and loudly slurs some complaints, they throw him in the Spanish clinker too, shaking their heads and muttering.

"Borrachos!"

Drunks.

And the Cookes are that and then some. They are perhaps Torremolinos' most celebrated drunken couple, the local non-literary equivalent of Zelda and F. Scott Fitzgerald. There's no *Gatsby El Grande*, just plenty of booze.

They can afford to live like this, he has inherited enough trust fund money that neither has to do a lick of work. They even have several maids to raise their two young sons.

And here they are free from the constraints of the strait-laced 1950's Eisenhower-era U.S. puritanical society they left back home.

And, as a local part of the living-in-limbo wild expatriate community, they are free from the daily moral and behavioral requirements of Catholic Spain.

So, *borrachos*? Well *porque no,* why not?

Plus, for a very few pesetas, the local wines and brandy taste damn good.

That is probably all the inspiration Bobbie needs for another one of her famous escapades: The *El Manaña* Caper.

The Cooke's large house off Calle San Miguel includes a big, private tree-lined garden with whitewashed walls. On the other side of the high back wall of their garden is the village's large open-air night club, the fancy *El Mañana*, where big bands play Latino music nightly as guests dine elegantly at their tables and dance the *merengue* under a canopy of towering trees covered with vines and creepers.

One special night, Bobbie is inspired by both alcohol and perhaps some particular African-based rhythm the *El Mañana* band's drummer is laying down.

So she climbs the wall of her garden, grabs hold of a vine, and from the top of the twelve foot high wall catches the attention of the nightclub dancers on the wall's other side with a bloodcurdling Tarzan yell.

"Aieeyaaeeeyaaaeeeyyaaa!!!"

Then she comes swinging on the vine over the startled dancers' heads like some kind of jungle-juice crazed she-ape, "You, Tarzan, Me, Bobbie".

Whomp!

She lands with a triumphant "Yahooooo!" right in the middle of somebody's formally set dinner table, sending glasses and plates full of food flying.

Now that's an entrance.

The Cookes are, on arrival, two more entries into the column of oddballs that have come to rock and shock this once peaceful, hard-working and straight-laced village. These are people who strangely don't seem to have to work at anything but having fun, something that must seem so odd in the eyes of simple hardworking Spanish villagers.

And the Cooke's are not alone in this odd parade.

There's also Steve and Armand. An American and a Frenchman, semi-retired interior decorators have set up an elaborately done up house in the sleepy *Bahondillo* fishing village, home otherwise of mostly poor, hard-working fishermen and campesinos.

And every local kid I know can tell you that this new couple is openly something very different.

"Mucho monkey."

And they are that, but only in this tiny part of Southern Spanish coast.

You see, local *andaluz* slang refers to *maricones* or gays as being "cute" or, in Spanish, *mono*.

Go to a Spanish-English dictionary, which some curious village kid must have done, and it will tell you the English word for *mono* is actually "monkey," as in the kind that swing in trees, not hang out in gay bars.

Consequently, all the village kids are mistakenly convinced that when you want to say someone is gay you say:

" You mucho monkey."

The traditional reply of "No. <u>You</u> mucho monkey," works but simply perpetuates this gay-simian misconception.

And Steve and Armand are *"monkey"*.

Mucho.

From a kid's point of view it's hard to say but they just don't walk, dress or talk like anybody we knew back in Chevy Chase did. Maybe it's the slim sandals and the brightly colored shirts and slacks, or the flamboyantly large straw hats and matching handbags, who knows. They get a lot of stares from the locals.

They are not alone in the monkey cage.

Passing through for an extended rest that first summer we are there, after the rigors of some Ivy League college, is a young man my mother and her girl friends archly refer to as "Sweet William", raising their eyebrows knowingly as they do.

"Sweet William" has first been to Rome where he got some special haircut he raves about where they carefully curled his black hair into ringlets like that of Caligula.

In Rome he also bought a spiffy, deluxe edition, silver and aluminum Lambretta scooter, one that's somehow too silvery shiny and gleamingly prissy to imagine any self-respecting local macho riding it.

But "Sweet William" does ride it everyday, arriving at the beach in leather Roman sandals and a shockingly skimpy bathing suit consisting of two tiny pieces of gold cloth, one for the front, one for the back, laced together in between by leather ties over naked skin.

Despite the fact that at the beach he is surrounded by cooing women, his whole act can openly be summed up in a few words.

"Very muchísimo monkey."

Not exactly in this full-monkey, faux simian category, but in the same fellow-traveler area, is an American Cafe owner called Rob Pauling. I hear the grownups refer to him as a "mama's boy," which apparently has something to do with the fact that, at forty or so, he still lives with his mother, and that she has the money propping up the cafe.

Unlike "Sweet William" and Steve and Armand, Rob likes girls in "that way" and even has a girlfriend, a pretty blonde Swiss lady, which is good as far as it goes.

One day as far as it goes is only halfway down the highway to Málaga, somewhere near the airport, when Bob's mother forces him to stop the car he's driving her and the girlfriend in.

Taking exception to something the Swiss girlfriend has said, the mother orders her out of the car and motions to Bob to slam the door and drive on, abandoning his Swiss Miss on the highway.

He does.

Momma's boys. Gays. World-class drunks. Vagrants and idlers.

Serial wife cheaters and/or swappers.

What a show the *extranjeros*, (foreigners, or even more accurately "strangers"), are putting on to entertain the locals.

In a hard-working, macho culture, the "strangers" are providing plenty of strange things to wag tongues about.

Plus, of course, there are all the affairs we overhear our mother and her friends gossip about. Who is sleeping with who's husband or wife, what rumored-to-be-gay bar owner is actually sleeping with that divorced lady from Chicago, what happened after that drunken party at the Cooke's. In a small village it all comes out in the day's gossip.

But not everything notable about the "strangers" is necessarily sordid. Some foreigners, like us, are basically just there for a fairly normal good time, so we pass mostly unnoticed. Others are remarkable because they are actually famous in the world for one reason or another.

For starters how about Ernest Hemingway. The author hangs around the area, notably in Málaga. My mother even meets him one time at a party in *Churriana* and he casually introduces her to a friend of his.

Ava Gardner.

Living quietly in the area are the actor Melvyn Douglas, one-time co-star to the likes of Greta Garbo, and his wife screenwriter Diana Douglas. They're not just there for a good time, they have been blackballed as Commies by the repugnant McCarthy led witch-hunt of the 1950's.

There's another Hollywood escapee rumored to be living way up in the mountain village of Mijas, supposedly keeping his wife, Lola, and their kids in a house so basic it even lacks running water. He's decided to chuck movies for now and pursue his original love of painting rather than to further become a celluloid household name.

Robert Redford.

Not that I'm all that interested in these people, I just overhear the grownups talking about this stuff that the *extranjeros* are getting up to. Then I go out and play with the extranjero kids.

In the summer there's a whole gang of us. Americans, Brits, Swedes and so on, changing almost weekly with the arrival and departure of parents eager to enjoy the sun and perhaps join in on the strangeness.

Those of us kids who are here more or less permanently establish a few rules. One of these is that any new kid who wants to be part of the gang and play with us has to first prove they are worthy by surviving a carefully prescribed centuries old Torremolinos ordeal dating back to the time of the Moorish kings.

The Cemetery Test.

We wait until dusk. The ominous shadows of night are darkening the lonely, dusty dirt road that leads out to the crest of the jagged rocks. Then the dark road continues along the lip of the cliff to the desolate whitewashed walls of the town cemetery.

At this hour nobody's around and a single bare light bulb weakly tries to illuminate the path halfway there.

After that, darkness.

There is a deathly silence broken only by the moan of wind in gnarled, old trees on top of the cliff and whistling through the graves of the departed.

The rules are simple.

The trembling, already frightened initiate is led to within twenty yards of the huge black iron gates that separate the land of the living from that of eternal death.

There we solemnly give them their final instructions.

"Walk up to the small door on the left of the black metal gate and touch it. Then, knock three times slowly."

"And wait for the dead to answer back."

Then they walk on alone in the gathering darkness to the very gates of *la Casa de los Muertos.*

The House of the Dead.

They knock three times on the massive iron gates, each knock echoing hollowly through the eerily silent tombstones.

Breathing hard and shaking with fear, they must wait to see if any dead spirit will answer their knock. They wait in the gloom and listen for the answer from beyond the grave.

"BROOOOOOOMMMMMM!'

Suddenly the main gates boom and roar with a wild crashing sound.

Torremolinos

The rest of us have hurled large rocks at the right side of the gate. They ricochet off the metal to hurl loud, booming metal echoes that swirl around the tombstones like howling ancient Moorish banshees looking for the blood of an innocent.

When our victim has recovers from the initial shock they turn back to ask us what's going on.

We are gone.

And they stand alone outside the house of *los muertos*.

We're running hard down the road, laughing hysterically, leaving the frightened initiate all alone in the dark and forbidding land of the eternal dead.

After that they are one of us.

Assuming, of course, they don't die of fright, which, surprisingly, none do. And there were plenty who lived through it over time.

We are put through it ourselves on arrival by David Stahl, a kid about my age from Sarasota, Florida.

His dad Ben is a commercial artist, one of the eight or so you read about in these ads in comic books that purport to test your artistic ability. The ads challenge you to draw a picture of a lady and send it in to try and gain admission to The Famous Artists School, which I imagine if you have the money is a done deal anyway.

But David's dad isn't in Spain to draw pictures of ladies in comic books. He's studying religious paintings and doing some oils of his own about various saints or something like that. Eventually back in Florida he will open some kind of religious art museum about the Bible My sister Mimi even poses for one of the paintings as a young lady mourning the death of the savior.

I have a cool time hanging out with David and, when he leaves, even get to buy his bike.

Also, his dad has this young college age apprentice guy, Greg, who forms an informal sort of scout group for ex-pat kids like us and takes us on hikes to the mountain tops or out to the *Rio Guadiana* at dawn.

Greg is a terrific young dude and we think he's totally cool because, when you check out his paintings and sketches at his studio apartment, you realize he gets to paint his girlfriend...totally nude.

Holy shit, is that cool or what?

When Greg isn't leading us, we tend to make up our own games, and lead the pack by ourselves, going on adventures to the mountain reservoir or pirate treasure hunts in the caves by the cliffs.

Or we learn you can make gunpowder with sulphur and chlorate bought at the local pharmacy, plus coal dust you make yourself. We make it in our laboratory, after which my brother Mark messes up a batch and blows his eyebrows off.

Hey, fun is where you find it.

For a period of time, a kid called Mackey lives in Torremolinos with his family that includes about eight younger children. With this ready-made troupe of gullible followers we concoct various fanciful adventures involving desperate robbers, Spanish highwaymen with hearts of gold or even space travelers.

One day we come up with the grandest adventure of them all.

"The Rocket to the Moon."

Using boxes and bits of wood, plus a metal fire pan with real fire in it, we construct an authentic, ultrasonic space rocket which we tell the wide-eyed group of kids we will take straight up to the moon.

This tries the imagination even of five and six years olds and the oldest of them, seven-year-old Petey, tells us so.

"That's just boxes and wood planks. You can't take that to the moon or anywhere."

Mark, Mackey and I shake our heads at disbelieving Petey and his foolish and ill-founded lack of faith in the power of science.

"Of course, we can. It's technologically designed for deep space travel," I assure them.

"Mackey and I will go first," my brother says, climbing in, then motions to me.

"David, better take the kids around the other side of the house, or the rocket's atomic blast will kill them."

As soon as I herd the protesting little kids out of harm's way, Mark and Mackey take the space rocket apart, concealing it's pieces in the garage. Then they hide inside the house and signal to me discreetly from the window. I turn to the kids.

"Hear that? They've rocketed off. Let's go watch them fly away."

We run back around the house and the little kids are awestruck to see the rocket gone. Maybe it really could go somewhere? Like maybe even the moon!

"There they go!" I point up at the sky "See them?"

One or two of the littlest ones nod uncertainly, though Petey says he can't at all see anything resembling a flying rocket.

After enough lunar exploration time goes by, like maybe five minutes, I look up and warn the anxiously waiting crowd of little ones.

"Quick! They're rocketing back. Get around to the other side of the house before the atomic blast scorches your brains to ashes!"

Once they're safely around the other side, Mark and Mackey emerge from the house to take the rocket from its hiding places, re-build it and sit down in it.

I send the kids running back around. Astonished to see the rocket again, they rush up to the intrepid spacemen.

"You're back! You're back! What was the moon like?"

"It was great! There's almost no gravity and you can hop around," the intrepid spacemen tell them.

Apparently they have bought it, although Petey still shakes his head suspiciously.

"Y-You're just tricking us."

"Alright," Mark says, putting his arm around Petey, "Will you believe us, will all of you kids believe us, if we take Petey here, who doesn't believe us, to the moon?"

"Yeah!" they chime in unison, even skeptical Petey agrees to the plan and sits in the rocket with Mark, readying to go, as I herd the little ones around the house and away from the atomic blast.

"I'm thirsty," Mark explains to the Petey, the lunar skeptic. "Let's get some water before we go. The moon's a long way off."

As soon as he takes Petey in the house, Mackey hides the rocket and I bring the little kids out to find the rocket gone.

They flip.

"They've gone, they've gone! Petey's really going to the moon!"

Inside the house, Mark delays Petey looking at some toys and also warns him about the hazards of "Lunar Amnesia".

It seems space travel is so tough on you, some weaker-minded first time travelers to the moon forget about some of it. Nothing to worry about though, probably won't happen to a strong guy like Petey, says Mark, surreptitiously slipping some rocks in Petey's blue jeans jacket.

Outside, I tell the kids the moon voyagers are returning and send them away. Quickly, Mackey rebuilds the rocket. Then Mark brings Petey back out to the rocket.

They sit down in it and prepare for blast off.

"All set, Petey? Okay, here we go."

As Petey braces for the atomic blast off, I cue the kids and they come racing around the house and up to the rocket.

"You're back, you're back! Tell us, Petey, what's the moon like, come on tell us!"

Totally befuddled, Petey looks around wildly.

"You were gone for a long time, Petey. What did you do on the moon?" a little one asks.

Mark jumps in. "We walked around and brought back some moon rocks. Petey has them in his jacket, right Petey?"

Even more puzzled, Petey reaches into his pockets and comes up with some rocks.

"It was really cool, wasn't it Petey?" says Mark peering intently at Petey's eyes.

"Say, you don't happen to have any of that "Lunar Amnesia" do you?"

"Me? Oh, uh, why no." Petey says uncertainly. "The moon.....the moon was cool."

I guess to the long litany of strange phrases you could use to describe the *extranjeros* in Torremolinos, we kids have just added one phrase probably even more appropriate for the adults.

" Lunatics."

David M. Johnson

6
Las escuelas

WHEN THAT FIRST GOLDEN SUMMER in Torremolinos reaches its end, workers begin taking down the brightly colored canvas awnings and thatched straw roofs from the beach cabanas, and shuttering up many restaurants and shops, closing the town down for the season.

The days grow cooler and the foreigners are all leaving as we soon will.

My brother Mark, my sister Mimi and I start to think ahead about the school year back in Chevy Chase.

Once again we'll enter the hallowed halls of Rosemary Elementary School to learn new and useful things, like last year's lesson in surviving a nuclear attack by Russia.

Apparently that can be accomplished by first hiding under your desk with your head covered by your arms, then marching down to the basement lunchroom to live off crackers and water stored in big barrels with triangular markings on them.

What happens after that and who comes to get us isn't made clear.

Whatever, it's school, but we will once again be back on familiar ground, on American soil, in *la tierra de* hamburgers and milk shakes and Mickey Mouse Club and Cub Scouts, after this brief and inexplicable interlude in the strange world called Spain.

I tell my friends we will be going back to *la escuela*, to school. Like all the other *turistas* we are going home as summer ends.

Home to America, apple pie, and, best of all, to our loving father. We can't wait to pack our bags and return.

That's when my mother drops the really big bomb on the three of us.

"Don't bother to pack. We're not going back."

What!?! Did we hear you right, lady?

"No. Not this fall", she says.

And, as far as we can get her to say, perhaps not ever. Maybe we are going to have to become Spaniards or something.

We are stunned. Shocked. Outraged.

We race through every possible range of emotion you can have as a kid who's suddenly, out of the blue, been told they are more or less permanently going to be cut off from civilization as they know it.

Torremolinos

We go through all the wild emotional stages, howling holy bloody murder at each one.

No more Mickey Mouse Club on TV, no *mas* cub scout baseball, no double decker burgers from the drive-in waitress at Hot Shoppes, no hot dogs no apple pie no Jerry Lewis movies with dad on weekends... wait a minute: <u>no dad</u>!

No way! This will not stand! Torremolinos is okay for a summer holiday but it is no place for American kids to call home, especially when all the tourists leave.

We will not allow it. Period. End of discussion.

But, of course, it does indeed stand. My mother has that one ultimate secret power anyone can wield against a kid. We're just the kids.

She's the grownup.

So she gets to say what's what. And that's that. She explains it so simply and so well:

"We're staying here. Because <u>we</u> actually like it better over here."

We vehemently shook our heads "no".

"We don't like it here".

It's maybe okay for a vacation, but clearly no place fit to live. It's shutting up for summer. The foreigners are all leaving. There is nothing here for us. No school, no activities, no friends.

Her reply is quite firm. "No. We like it better here. You just need some time to realize it."

She looks away smiling and examines her fingernails, like some cat looking at its sharp claws, and pronounces the conversation over.

"We like it better here. And that's all there is to it."

In truth, the one "we" that mattered in this decision does really like it much better in Torremolinos.

For my mother, still young and attractive in her thirties, there is a constant whirl of parties and trips with exotic new

75

found friends, suitors and lovers. While, having left my father for someone else and a second marriage that quickly failed, the court awarded her no alimony from our father to live on nor was there any from the brief other marriage

But for her there's a golden lining here in Spain. Our father does send court-ordered generous child support to pay for the education and upbringing of the three of us kids.

With that child support money from Dad firmly in her grasp in Spain our mother discovers a personal paradise.

She is able to rent nice villas and have a full-time maid to cook, clean and tend to the children, even have her clothes tailor-made by a *modista* in Málaga who copies things from fashion magazine pages my mother rips out and shows her.

It's like that Chevy Chase divorce court judge actually did award her alimony....on jet propelled after burners.

All without having to do a lick or work. If that's the deal, what woman wouldn't like it better here in Torremolinos? As long as you gloss over the little fact that you do have kids to take care of, educate and think about.

But who says you have to do that?

That fall to demonstrate to us children how much "we" like living 5,000 miles away from America and our dad, she takes us on trips to Morocco and Granada. There, in these strange places, she gushes happily to us what lucky kids we are to actually be here.

"None of those kids in America get to see all this! You're experiencing other cultures!"

And so begins a series of near daily lectures on what fortunate children we are to be living in "Europe", a word she always pronounces with special emphasis, as if it were perhaps some place akin to "Heaven". We are constantly reminded how lucky we are that she has brought us here to give us all that this wonderful new world has to offer.

"Europe!"

Lest we dare to forget our good fortune.

Our mother snaps our photos in the *souk* at Tangier and in the Courtyard of the Lions in Granada's Alhambra Palace, all the while drilling into us how super lucky we are to be here, instead of that boring old useless America that nobody cares about anyway.

Some fifty years later my sister discovers those photos and sends them to me. They make me incredibly sad.

In these faded black and white snapshots, with my brother wearing an ill-fitting fez, I see three unsmiling, very puzzled children. They dimly realize their lives have just been royally screwed by the yakking lady with the camera but don't quite understand how.

If we fully realized the extent of our loss, we
probably would be crying in those pictures.

We have just had ripped away from us any real contact with a father who loves us and cares for us. Also taken away is interaction with any of our family and friends in America.

We become strangers to them. Ghosts to our family and to our own home country of America.

Soon they exist for us only as memories that grow dimmer with each year, like old fading photographs. Over time we lose our past and our American roots wither away, like the bone dry shards of a dying tree.

Gone also is the opportunity to grow up as part of the culture we will ultimately, as Americans, struggle to belong to. When we finally return we will feel like clueless foreign geeks, stumbling around dazed and confused, strangers in a world strange to us.

And, not having any Spanish family or connection, we will not be invited to be part of that culture either.

The "other culture" we are going to "experience", a perk my mother constantly promises us lucky kids will have, is actually the highly sketchy ex-patriate world.

From years of experience with it, I don't recommend it.

And we are about to be educated, if you can call it that, by a patchwork hodgepodge of sub-standard stop-gaps. By college time, it will leave me admitted nowhere, unfocused and confused.

My siblings and I will also never experience the benefits of participating in organized activities particularly sports, something from having my own kids I know is an invaluable character building experience, learning to work with a team, to use strategy, to win and lose, to gain self esteem.

Even though, according to my German American grandmother Phyllis Wagner, of Pittsburgh, we are related to Hall of Fame baseball great Honus Wagner of the Pirates, I have no idea if I am any good at baseball.

Or football. Or basketball for that matter. Or anything your normal American kids expects as his or her birthright.

Nope. No America stuff for you, pal.

But all that pales, next to having our father taken away from us.

He is the loving Dad we depend on to be there for us every Sunday. He takes us to Jerry Lewis and Dean Martin movies, or Glen Echo amusement park, the Ice Capades or Ringling Brothers circus.

Afterwards there is Chinese food, or hamburgers at the Hot Shoppes, or spaghetti with meatballs at his Italian favorite restaurant.

And, at the end of the day when he drops us off, he hugs us and tells us how much he loves us.

Hugs and expressions of love are two things absolutely not in our mother's repertoire. She never doles out either.

Instead of hugs and the "L" word, now she gives us "We like it better here!"

With that simple phrase my mother takes away all the marbles. And Dad, too.

Why he never came to visit us and rescue us I don't know to this day.

Perhaps having re-married and with two new daughters, plus a demanding job, he has his plate full and figures our mother had us covered. I just don't know.

On that trip to Morocco, which my mother takes us on to show us how wonderful our new world is, I get my own personal glimpse at how special our new lives will actually be.

On the ferry from Algeciras to Tangier, a young blond German guy somehow attaches himself to my mother. She seems to enjoy his company, laughing at every thing he says. We kids are uneasy.

After checking in at our hotel, we go to see the *souk*, or teeming marketplace. And there the young German is again, attached to my mother's side like some kind of a Kraut suckerfish.

We plunge into the *souk's* eerie labyrinthine warren of stalls and shops, stopping here and there to go in. In one dark store I am fascinated by an ornately decorated Moorish dagger on a table.

When I look up from the dagger, the store is empty save for the grinning shop keeper, everyone I'm with has vanished: Mimi, Mark, my mother, and the blond German suckerfish.

I go out to the alley outside the shop, but can't find them in any of the stores. I try the next alley. And the next. I go back to the original street where I last saw them. Nothing. I try another alleyway.

Soon I am hopelessly lost in the vast and strange *souk*. In the searing North African heat I look vainly for someone who speaks English

I am afraid. I have heard things about Arabs stealing children never to be seen again. I begin crying as I wander, the hot sun beating down merciless and deaf to the sobbing of a little ten-year-old American boy.

Strange people try to sell me things in languages I can't understand. It is all a senseless babble with the searing sun beating down.

I become convinced I am going to die alone in this strange place. The Morrocan's will slit my throat and kill me.

I wander like this for hours until, somehow, I by chance take a road up out of the market to a palm tree-ringed plaza where I recognize with relief our hotel.

The front desk gives me our room key and I go up and collapse on the bed, exhausted and played out, falling into a deep sleep.

I awake to the click of the key being turned and the room door opening.

My mother comes in and spots me on the bed.

"David! You're here!"

I want to tell her how frightened I have been, what has happened, how much I cried and how I thought I was going to die. I want her to hug me and say everything will be okay.

"Whack!"

Her first blow sends my head smacking against the white plaster wall. The next one slams me into the headboard. She pummels me with both hands, hard.

"How dare you run away like that! You thoughtless and selfish little shit! You ruined everyone's afternoon!"

"How dare you run away you little unthinking brat!"

As the blows continue I try to hide by scrambling under the wood writing desk against the wall. Grabbing me by the ankles, she hauls me out roughly and continues to rain blows on me as I try to protect my head with my arms.

"Don't!" SMACK! "Ever!" WHAP! "Run!" WHOMP! "Away!" SMACK! "Again!" WHAP!

For a moment the blows stop. I peer out from under my arms. The room is empty. A second later, she emerges from the bathroom, her face contorted with anger, clutching by the handle a clear plastic hair brush with hard nylon bristles.

I recognize this. She only reserves that brush for times I am particularly bad and she is insanely enraged, like the times I've said bad words and she has to wash my mouth out with soap, then use the nylon bristle hairbrush. And she has a special way of making sure it really hurts, so the lesson sinks in.

She throws me roughly over her knees as she sits on a chair, yanks down my shorts and underpants, and begins to smack my bare bottom.

With each successive stinging whack she builds to an angry crescendo.

"Never!....Run!.....Away!.....Again!"

That last whack is so hard she breaks the hard hair brush handle.

Her rage mostly spent and the brush broken anyway, she turns to go, first ordering me confined to the room as punishment for naughtily "running away" and ruining everyone's afternoon fun, presumably even the vanished Kraut suckerfish's amorous plans. He's vanished.

Out the open window, I can hear my brother and sister play happily that afternoon in the hotel pool.

Because I selfishly "ran away" I am not allowed to swim there for the rest of our stay but must stay in my room.

Welcome to your new world, kid. Same as your old world, mom occasionally flips out and gets the hairbrush. Only Dad's now an ocean away. There's no phone you can pick up and call him.

And nobody speaks your language. Those are your cards. Deal with it.

I resign myself to this "wonderful" new world and whatever it brings next.

Can't wait.

Back in Torremolinos, we prepare to see what life after summer, in a town empty of tourists, brings us.

If we thought it through carefully during our anguished secret protest meetings against the evil authority, we might realize there is at least one silver lining in our situations from a kid's perspective.

There is no place to send us to school. *No escuelas.*

Think about it. After four months there our Spanish isn't in any way fluent enough to go to whatever local public schools there were, even if they would admit us.

I mean, it isn't like they had established special bilingual classes for deserving children of tourists. They probably don't even have bilingual options back then in California for Spanish speakers, much less in Spain for a handful of *americanos* and other international flotsam and jetsam.

And, guess how many special schools for foreigners there are in the area?

Zippo. *Nada.*

Ergo, ipso facto, no *escuela* for us.

Once we realize this key fact, being sentenced to life in Torremolinos doesn't seem quite so bad. Given a choice of school or no school most children will quickly tell you the second option's the more fun choice.

It's what we call today a no-brainer, at least from a juvenile perspective.

Of course, my mother makes a number of half-hearted attempts over the time that we are there to see that we don't end up like those kids in Pinocchio who make the mistake of going to the land of permanent play and wind up with donkey ears.

And, whether it is through her efforts or much more likely just plain dumb luck, not one of the three of us has actually ended up a braying jackass.

I know my sister and brother aren't and, unless people are keeping something really big from me like Jim Carrey in the movie "Truman," I don't think I am either. We can all read and write. We went to college. We haven't joined the Communist Party or the John Birch Society or the Tea Party or the Moonies or been convicted of felony crimes.

We don't own assault rifles or even plan to. We're kind of normal. Well, we certainly would be if there actually were such a thing.

Back then in Torremolinos one of the first options my mother tries with Mark and me actually is kind of a local private school, a sort of a one room class for village boys whose parents can afford to pay a bit.

It's upstairs in the building just down from Crazy Man's house. I think the guy who runs it speaks some English, at least I remember a few halting phrases from him, and so he must have convinced my mother he could therefore possibly give us some kind of education.

Or maybe she thinks it will be sort of like that sink or swim approach you're supposed to try at swimming pools: throw the kids into the deep end with a bunch of Spanish kids and maybe we'll choke a bit and then come back up to the surface sputtering in fluent Spanish and swim off doing the Andalusian backstroke.

Whatever.

I remember the professor is some kind of half midget, with maybe a little hunchback thrown in for good measure.

He rides up on one of those putt-putting red Guzzi motorbikes, dismounting with a strict air of authority, head held high, speaking not a word to any of the waiting students.

In the classroom, the midget teacher strides about fingering a waxy black moustache under a large colored-in photograph of his *Excelentisímo El Generalísimo Francisco Franco*. Perhaps it's a cousin of the similar photos in the barbershop, the post office, the banks, etc. It seems His Most Excellence Franco is everywhere and he has even followed us to school.

And, this is a new one for us, the mini professor has the nail of his little finger grown about two inches long so he can use it to flick the ash off his ever present cigarillo (cheap black Celtas, I believe).

He sits there talking about Cervantes or Lope de Vega or some strange math we know nothing about. Mark and I nod back at him uncomprehendingly in this class full of local boys who probably don't get it either, and the professor reaches out with that yellowed long little fingernail and flick, flick, flicks the ashes of his cigarette onto the floor.

One day I understand him enough to get that he is covering the historic naval battle of Trafalgar. I basically learn that a greatly outnumbered but plucky Spanish fleet inflicted heavy casualties on the vast English fleet, commanded by Admiral Nelson and that, though technically defeated, Spain basically won the day.

Some years later during a brief period of school at Wandsworth public school in London, the English history professor explains that at Trafalgar, it was actually a vastly outnumbered but plucky British fleet that took on the mammoth Spanish one and, though Nelson died, Britain won the day.

Those two differently skewed tellings of the same story in two different countries are one of the best history lessons I ever have.

Come to think of it, the lesson they really teach applies pretty accurately to a lot of ordinary life. Who won the day? And who was the goat?

Depends who's telling the story.

Upstairs in our one room Spanish school, it quickly becomes apparent that one of the micro teacher's privileges, besides flicking cigarette ashes with his yellow fingernail, is that he can whack kids with his ruler, hard, and he is kind of mean about it.

If you make a mistake during class it is duly noted on a sheet of paper. Then, at the end of class, all the miscreants have to stand in line and one by one get their knuckles sharply rapped by the midget man before he rides off proudly on his sputtering little red moto.

Anyway, that doesn't last long. I guess it is obvious to all parties we aren't going to learn Spanish overnight and go swimming fluently off in those particular Mediterranean waters of scholasticism.

Our little sister Mimi is very lucky our mother doesn't sentence her to the one girl's schooling option available: a Catholic convent boarding school in Málaga run by very strict nuns.

Two California ex-pat girls we meet our second winter there, Ceci and Laurie, aren't so fortunate. Their mother Rhoda brings them from California to Torremolinos, rents a nice villa, then sends the girls off Sunday evening to Friday night to this nun run boarding school miles away in Málaga.

For just $30 a month (second girl 10% off) this leaves mom scot free all week to enjoy the wild ex-pat party scene in Torremolinos down the road from the cold Málaga convent.

In order for her girls to pass their entrance interview with the nuns, Rhoda reasons that being a divorced mother in Catholic Spain won't pass muster. So she gives the girls instructions. The nuns ask them "And what about your father, dears?" The girls have the politically correct answer ready.

"He died. In the war."

"Oh, you poor little things!"

They're in.

And dad is dead.

Though as a US Marine Corps officer he's very much alive for years, even eventually as a commander at the marine training base at Quantico, Virginia.

Younger Ceci, 12, seems to take convent life in stride, years later even remembers that she learns to skip rope for the first time with the Spanish girls and enjoys that in particular.

However Laurie at 14 is devastated. Back before Spain, when they live in La Jolla, California, she gets a taste of US high school life: football games, parties, dating, freedom and an older surfer boyfriend her mother heartily disapproves of.

By contrast in the Spanish convent Laurie gets: Jesus three hours a day on her knees on the stone floor of the vast cathedral; strict silence during their meals; total separation from her sister, the only other English speaker there; a Spanish language she has never studied, and, since she doesn't speak Spanish she isn't deemed fit to study for college and is put on the *secretariada* track for future secretaries. Typing and dictation and embroidery it is, for Laurie.

Plus of course those all important classes on the history of the Catholic Church, god knows little kids need that.

When Rhoda asks the younger Ceci what she is getting out of school, the girl glumly replies: "Square knees," referring to the three hours a day kneeling before the holy altar.

They also get a hard bed in curtained off cubicles in a shared dormitory where Laurie cries herself to sleep every lonely night, her high school glory days in California a fading memory.

There are it seems worse fates than the Johnson kids own school-less predicament.

One weekend when Ceci and Laurie are back from their convent prison, they cause a local sensation when they brazenly dare to walk down *Calle San Miguel*....in colorful Madras Bermuda <u>shorts</u>.

Women aren't supposed to wear pants at all in Spain back then and certainly not short ones that show legs and knees. What may have been common casual wear in La Jolla, California, gets startled stares from the townsfolk here in Torremolinos.

Qué barbáridad! Qué escándalo!!!

Finally, several random events free Ceci and Laurie from the grasp of the strict nuns and the father, son and Holy Ghost in the cold and lonely Málaga convent.

First, Ceci begins to lose weight partly because of the poor food and partly because the nuns insist the girls eat absolutely everything properly with a knife and fork.

"Have you ever tried eating an orange with a knife and fork?" she tells me years later. "I stopped eating and was getting thinner."

The nuns begin to suspect the little American girl has worms and therefore might pose a health threat to the other girls.

Then the Sisters discover that older sister Laurie has brought to the convent and shared with the other girls a copy of San Diego Life magazine. It is full of pictures of young women in (God forbid!) bathing suits and shorts.

The nuns instinctively know that young ladies showing their alluring bare legs is not proper fashion but something evil conceived by Satan himself.

Vile pornography.

The magazine is confiscated. And surely burned.

Perhaps the final straw is when mom Rhoda is startled to hear Laurie, her former surfer girl daughter, muse about what it might be like to go through life as a nun.

"I wonder what it would feel like to give myself to Jesus," the teen tells her mother.

Suddenly, the convent thing is out.

No más Jesús.

The American girls are forced to spend all their time in Torremolinos with the rest of us international orphans, a fate they happily embrace.

We're happy, too. We get two added friends to play with and, because they are from California, they seem a connection somehow to the almost by now mythical America we have been separated from.

Laurie and Ceci are around that Christmas and help us feel more anchored to the jolly holidays we are used to back in America.

That isn't an easy thing in Torremolinos.

Spain in the late 1950's doesn't seem to have got the Christmas idea America has. There aren't Christmas trees everywhere. Or anywhere at all really. Somehow our mother manages to obtain a scraggly little pine tree and we decorate it with what we can, stringing pop corn kernels onto a thread to make white garlands.

Nowhere in town do you hear any of the familiar Christmas songs, no Nat King Cole crooning about "chestnuts roasting under an open fire", no hearty choruses belting out "God Rest Ye Merry Gentlemen."

Yes, groups of kids do come around singing Christmas songs. But they are called "*villancicos*" and they aren't about Santa Claus and his reindeer or white Christmases or any of that familiar stuff.

They accompany these strange songs with the "Thwonka-thwonka" of a rhythmic drum called a *zambomba*. It's like a long ceramic drum with a goat skin stretched on the top. Stuck in the middle of that skin is a thin reedy stick. You wet your hand with water, grip the stick and rub your hand up and down on it and out comes this odd sound. *Zambombas* just ain't happening during Christmas in Bethesda. We are surely on some other planet for this holiday.

Also, these caroling kids aren't expecting to be rewarded with steaming cups of hot chocolate. They want money, honey. Here in Spain, apparently Christmas is for sale.

Through her connections to the US airmen at Rota Naval base, Ceci and Laurie's mom Rhoda manages to come up with, thanks to the base PX grocery store, a massive US style turkey and some cranberry sauce.

One problem: this gargantuan American bird is far too large to fit in the little Spanish coal-fired ovens in any of our houses. So our Christmas turkey gets baked, along with the local bread and *tortas* in the large oven of the local *panaderia*, the town bakery on *Calle Miguel Angel.*

Together so far from America, we little band of *Americanos* put together a patchwork Christmas as best we can. I imagine we are sort of like Davy Crockett and his frontier family, way out in the unfamiliar wilderness, banding together to stitch a Christmas out of what the wild woods have to offer, like maybe acorns and baked squirrel meat and Christmas stockings stitched from rawhide.

And in Spain, who's going to stuff all those stockings anyway? Not Santa, my friend, there is no Santa Claus in 1950's Spain.

Whaaaaaat?!!

Come again. What's that you say?!!

No Santa Claus, ixnay on that. No jolly fat man, no flying sleigh, no Rudoph and Prancer and Dancer and so on!?! That is batshit crazy!

You want crazy? Okay I'll give you crazy, man.

How about you get don't presents on Christmas morning?! You don't get n*ada* until January 7! Try that on for crazy.

But wait. There's more.

To make it even more insane, Santa Claus doesn't bring the presents.

The Three Kings do.

Wait!

What Three Kings are you talking about?

You know the "We Three Kings of Orient are, tried to smoke our father's cigar"....you know them?

Yeah.

Those Three Kings.

Holy Moly. No presents on Christmas Day. And no Santa. Just Three Kings! Three....,flipping....Kings!

Toto, we are not in Kansas anymore.

That's the kind of Christmas we Johnsons from Bethesda and our little California girl *compadres* discover is ours.

Having other stranded American friends like Laurie and Ceci around somehow makes our exile from the home we love a little easier to endure.

One day when our parents are all galivanting who knows where, 14-year-old Laurie, the oldest and most knowledgeable of our little group, decides to let a whole group of us younger expat brats in on a little secret she's heard about.

She gives us the "birds and bees" talk in full detail. Like the what is this "sex" thing lesson.

I'm like, wow, who knew all that?

Back before all this, when we are still in Bethesda in the good old USA and I'm maybe seven years old, our mother one day mutters something vague about the subject of "you need to know how babies happen" and then, too embarrassed to go on any further, hands us a little illustrated book and retreats to her bedroom.

Mark, Mimi and I study the drawings with very mild curiosity.

Some illustrations seem to be about a man's "thing" and a woman's "thing", but it's all very sterile and scientific looking in black and white illustrations. There are charts and graphs. It seems to us that making babies is like a science experiment.

Another drawing shows a man and woman smiling with happy nurses in the hospital, the wife is in a wheelchair, and I come away with the mistaken notion for years that in order to make a baby you had to both somehow get into wheelchairs, the nurses might wheel you together and then somehow you proceed to, scientifically of course, do "it".

Soon getting bored with this, we kids put the book away and I am left with this hazy wheelchairs = sex = babies notion.

In Torremolinos, teenage Laurie sweeps away all the confusion and tells us the real low down, the "no wheelchairs" version, the one the older, more experienced teens in California told her about. She also leaves us with this refreshingly novel idea she's also been told: making babies is not so much a cold science project but that sex is actually lots of fun and feels incredibly good and people really, really enjoy it.

I am grateful to this day for that lesson. Thanks so very much for setting me right, Laurie. That's been good to know.

There are a small group of other kids in town who are in the same boat we all are. Americans, English, Swedish, Irish, etc. Other parents are in the same predicament: how can you go out on the town and to the Bar Central, have parties and affairs and fun when there's this nagging thought that you forgot one minor detail: your children aren't getting an education.

Oops, aren't parents supposed to see to that?

Independently, some of us kids find our own ways to educate ourselves about the world. For my brother Mark, it becomes going to the movies to learn about life from the silver screen.

For me it's books. They are my escape and my teacher.

Cut off from the world I knew, I intuitively become a bookworm. I devour every book I can get my little hands on, plundering the bookshelves of all the ex-pats we know.

My brother and sister and even our mother make fun of the fact my face is always buried in a book, I ignore their mean teasing and read on.

From a British lady friend of our mothers, I get the entire Penguin book series of the fabulous English writer John Master's historical series set in India, tracing generations of the Savage family. I am mesmerized by the exotic world of "The Deceiver's", the scary "Night Runner's of Bengal", the heart break of "Bhowani Junction" and so much more.

I even force myself through some Tolstoy, Dostyyevski and Checkov, not liking them too much, but doing it because I have read they are important writers and I want to see what they have got.

I discover Hemingway and read everything of his I can get my hands on. The same with John Steinbeck, I plunge into their worlds with delight, leaving my exile temporarily for the writer's stories.

Norman Mailer, James T. Farrell's "Studs Lonigan" trilogy, Stephen Crane, James Fenimore Cooper, Mark Twain, Washington Irving's "Tales of the Alhambra", Charles Dickens, Emile Zola, Lope De Vega, all the way to Micky Spillane and Dashiel Hammet, and a heady slew of Science Fiction, I race my way from bookshelf to bookshelf, back and forth in time, country to country, eager to taste whatever is next.

All these beautiful authors, I credit them today for teaching me by their example, and by sheer osmosis, to be the professional writer I am today. Since leaving university with a journalism degree, I've paid the rent with my pen, first as a journalist, then an ad man, and now whatever.

Back then in Torremolinos those writers were my rescuers and my true educators, making up for the lack of any other worthwhile ones. They were all I had.

There may have been grownups in Torremolinos who are so far gone into the party life they didn't care about their kids education and reasoned children could tend pretty well to themselves.

But for most parents, the stock phrase that "Our kids are going to be so much more broadened by having lived abroad, " (Get it? Living *"abroad"* makes you more *"broadened"*, whatever that is). Sounds more like something a steady diet of super-sized McDonald's , Cheetos, and Coke will do to your body. This phrase doesn't dispel that nagging doubt for some parents that they are not fulfilling their educational parental duties.

So an apparent solution arises.

The somewhat hefty French grande dame who has the Berlitz language teaching franchise in the area announces that she will run a school for little foreign kids, unofficially under the well-known Berlitz imprimatur no less.

So we try that next.

Imagine this poor lady, used to dealing with polite grownups eager to learn the smatterings of French or Italian or Spanish, having instead to deal with a roomful of international brats who basically don't want to be there in the first place.

It just wasn't fair, there was no way she is equipped to deal with this kind of thing.

Other than those few times when we boys suddenly behave like little gentlemen because we are sent to another room to learn French from the comely young French woman in her employ, already the subject of many of our erotic imaginations, other than that, the whole thing is chaos.

I think we spend most of our time playing outside in the garden while the Berlitz lady recuperates from having to deal with the lot of us by sipping a soothing glass of sherry.

Our mother also makes a feeble attempt to have us properly schooled in *España* by having us use a series of scholastic workbooks duly sent from America. By diligently working through these and by completing and grading the enclosed tests faithfully, we will end up thoroughly educated.

Big problem: who is going to make us diligently and faithfully do all this stuff?

Our mother's not sticking around to make us do it. She's got a world of adventure out there beckoning to her. Trips to make. Things to buy. Dresses to get made. Men to dally with.

So, on her way out the door, with a ladylike wave of her hand, she instructs the maid to make us kids sit down and see that we study our workbooks all morning.

As if.

Once our *madre* is out of sight, we run out the door, past the maid vainly begging us to do our schoolwork, and explore whatever the day had in store for us.

No, the workbook thing does not work.

And so after well over two years with no real schooling of any kind we arrive at Reiner.

Picture this madly grinning German guy wearing sandals, eyes slightly bugged out, blond hair curly and long, way back before any men we knew wore long hair.

He walks up to you and shakes your hand firmly and says in this heavy German accent: "Hello, I ahm Rye-nah, I vill be your tutah. Ve vill learn many things, yah?"

Then, he drags you off to his digs way up in the Calvario village on the hill above the town, practically up in the mountains, high above where any people you actually know live. But it's okay because he drags your brother Mark and sister Mimi along.

"Reiner is really smart," my mother had tells us. "He's a genius. His whole family is. His brother's the conductor of the Leipzig orchestra."

Oh, why didn't you tell us in the first place, mom: The Leipzig orchestra? That changes everything. We'll gladly go and learn from this weird-looking, long-haired, sandal-wearing, freaky guy whose country not too long ago was our sworn enemy.

Yeah, sure.

You know what, Reiner isn't so bad.

In fact, he is actually very good. We learn things, or at least I remember I did. He has this way of making you concentrate on the work really hard, so hard I remember actually crying that I can't do the math, but he is never mean.

And when you get it and are good, you get a cookie from his cache in the cookie tin beneath the pot-bellied stove.

Or, if the weather is warm you get to take a break and get to swim in the small pool at his bungalow complex.

Despite the tears of frustration, I master algebra with him that I won't meet again till high school. Maybe if I'd had other math teachers like that, I wouldn't be a writer today, but a mathematician.

Then again, knowing me, maybe not.

But anyway, we like him, behind the sandals and the weird hair, he is a nice guy and probably the only real teacher we found in Torremolinos.

Which doesn't at all explain the motives, if there are any besides the usual childish mischievousness, behind a sad chapter in U.S.-German relations.

"The Raid On Reiner's".

It happens a bit later in our Torremolinos years when he is no longer our tutor.

Torremolinos

We are being schooled in England for brief spells, but are back in Torremolinos for the summer. We have rented a big house with a garden, right in the *Bahondillo*, just past the fishermen's houses.

For some reason my brother decides that the thing for us to do, us meaning he, our friend Dana and me, is to conduct a clandestine "Raid On Reiner's". To really pillage the place, ransack and lay waste because, I don't know, just because.

I remember that the Nazi thing was mentioned frequently but I guess it is really in the end just plain old adolescent hijinks. Besides Reiner is Jewish, kind of squelches the whole Nazi angle.

All day long we plan and plot and, at dinner, we exchange secret, meaning-filled glances.

Tonight, Reiner gets it.

Dinner done, we gather our plucky little band of raiders in the streets of the Bahondillo, then head up the steps that wind up the cliff, past the ruins of the old watchtower, through the main part of town, the Calle San Miguel packed with strollers doing their evening *paseo*, all peacefully oblivious to our dangerous and secret mission.

As we head up the hill, past the market, we spot Reiner happily coming down, totally ignorant of the hammer that is about to come down on his German High Command Sanctuary.

From the shadows we watch and, knowing he is gone probably to the Bar Central for hours, we quicken our pace. The way is clear, the German SS sentries are momentarily distracted, the prize is unguarded and within sight.

Once there we make quick work of his bungalow. Out from its hiding place under a rock comes the key, and into the German headquarters itself go the four daring American commandos, intent on spreading havoc and ruin.

Had we planted satchel bombs and *plastique*, the destruction cannot be more complete. All the books come down from the shelves. The chimney is stuffed with leaves so that when he starts a fire, smoke will billow back into the German command post. Clothes are strewn about.

And, sacrilege of sacrilege, out came the hidden cookie tin and we triumphantly gorge on the cookies that had previously been parsimoniously doled out one by one after tedious academic slaving, laughing so hard that pieces of cookie come spouting out of our mouths, scattering onto the red tile floor.

Then, for the piece de resistance, we haul his mattress off his bed and with a ho-heave ho fling it into the swimming pool where it lands with a massive "kersploosh!"

Our work done, the destruction complete, we carefully put the key back into its hiding place and swagger down the hill, back down the dirt road towards the center of town, chortling and congratulating ourselves in the darkness on our mission success.

"I can't wait till he finds out about it," my brother Mark loudly crows.

From the dark road ahead, a voice booms out. "Can't wait till who finds out about what?"

A few steps more and, to our horror, we can see the voice has a familiar owner.

"Run! It's Reiner!"

We scream and flee in panic, busted, running desperately all the way through town, down the cliff side steps to the *Bahondillo* and our respective houses, arriving totally out of breath, hearts pounding.

My mother notices that we are back from our stroll about town later than usual, but other than that notices nothing out of the ordinary as we creep guiltily off to bed, our minds racing through the possible outcomes.

Maybe Reiner won't put two and two together. Maybe he'll think it was some nasty *Calvario* kids or even burglars. Maybe we'll get away with it, I remember hoping and thinking as I lie in bed.

A sudden angry pounding on the door downstairs and a man's raised voice tells me otherwise. It is followed by the sound of heavy footsteps coming up the stairs as we cower under our covers.

That's when I jump from under the blanket and quickly hide under my bed on the cool tile floor.

From my vantage point I see Reiner's sandal clad feet, hear shouting and harsh words as he seizes my brother and makes him get dressed and go off into the night with him. Mercifully, cowering and holding my breath in the darkness by the wall under my bed, nobody finds me.

Hours later, Mark comes back, soaking wet.

Reiner has hauled him all the way back to his ravaged house and forces him to clean up every bit of the destruction.

Then, Reiner leads him to the swimming pool. There is a dark object floating in it. "Mark," Reiner asks, "Can you tell me vat dat is over dere?"

"Uh....your mattress?"

"Zat's right, Reiner replies. "Now, go get it."

With a shove Mark goes in, fully clothed.

Maybe it's fitting my brother gets the brunt of the punishment (although there is some house arrest for us all), as my memory is that it was Mark's plan in the first place to conduct this raid on our former teacher.

In retrospect, while I rather relish the memory of "The Raid On Reiner's", it still isn't life at its fairest.

If any of our teachers deserved a little punishment, maybe it was the little midget Spanish guy with the long fingernail who used to rap our knuckles, not the rather kind German who actually managed to teach a few ungrateful American brats a thing or two.

But, I guess kids don't always learn their lesson immediately. Sometimes they only get them years later.

In the *escuela* of hard knocks .

Torremolinos

7

La Señora

EVERYBODY GETS A NICKNAME.

This is one of the various unwritten rules of life in Torremolinos, at least among the kids.

Your nickname may mean something specific like *"El Loco"* (The Crazy One) or *"El Cojo"* (The One With The Limp).

But more often it's just an "el" or a "la" (male or female) added before some local retranslation of your name.

The local kids look at you, size you up, and clap a moniker on you.

So, as David or Davey, I become *"El Daybe."* Mark or "Marcos" becomes *"El Miko,"* (pronounced like "Mike-oh") and my sister Mimi becomes very simply *"La Mimi."*

That's how the local kids refer to you. If they see you coming they say to each other:

"Allí viene El Daybe." (There comes "The Davey"). And so on, etc..

Somewhere very quickly after we get there, we American kids decide it's only fair that the rule be applied to our mother. And that she roundly deserves to get one of those nicknames that carry extra special meaning.

So, we dub her what all the maids we have over time call her:

"La Señora"

That's "The Lady", as in "The Lady of the House."

For us it carries several meanings. Of course, there's the "Lady of The House" nonsense, as such it's a term of respect, often from someone more lowly and subservient who you pay to call you that.

And, who can be more lowly back then in Spain than a maid you pay meager wages to and refer to as your *"chica"* or your "girl"? Kind of like back in the bad old slave days calling your grown black servant man a "boy."

Only in Spain your "boy" is a grown up woman. The *"chica"*.

I'm sure some of the *chicas* were surprised and shocked by seeing some of the things these *extranjeros* were up to. The affairs, the drinking, not having to work at all must seem inconceivable to those who have to work so hard for so very little.

Our young California friends Ceci and Laurie really notice this when their mother Rhoda makes the acquaintance in a bar of some young sailors from the US Navy base at Rota. She invites them over for dinner and they arrive with Spanish dates.

The maids are outraged, recognizing the "dates" as local girls of ill repute for hire by anyone with money.

Even a lowly *"chica"* isn't supposed to talk with a *"puta"*, much less serve a dinner to local whores.

In 1957, you pay your "girl" $12-15 a month to work six days a week living in, with only Sunday off. And this fully grown "girl" is required to bow and scrape and call you *"La Señora"* or "The Lady".

And that becomes our mother's nickname.

For us kids the sharper meaning of calling our mother *"La Señora"* is in the mockery area of utter disrespect and covert rebellion against an oppressor. While it sounds like a term of respect it was actually what today we call a "dis".

So referring to your mother as *"La Señora"*, you can be cocking your snoot at someone who puts on unnecessary airs, acting the Grand Lady and swanning about, simply because in this poor country she can afford a maid.

Or you can be complaining about someone who orders people, especially little children people, about, secretly dissing someone who decides you'll remain as a prisoner without walls in a country you never actually chose to be in or want to.

Now that's a good nickname.

And what of this..."Lady*?* "

Why you might ask would a divorced suburban housewife with kids but no real career, one who'd never traveled extensively outside the US, why would she suddenly pick up house and move to a strange country where she had no relatives, no job, didn't speak the language and knew absolutely no one?

I mean, it's not like there's even a drop of Spanish blood in *La Señora.*

Her parents are German and Welsh and they divorce when she is very young. She grows up in Rye, New York, the

Waspy suburbs of Westchester, not the gypsy barrio de la Triana in Sevilla.

Not very *español*.

And her childhood during The Depression is difficult, not the least because her father loses all his money and job and her parents divorce.

As a kid myself I have no inkling of this. But many decades later, as an adult, I piece together enough things I see and hear to realize that our mother has a tough, abusive childhood, and that she emerges from it emotionally scarred, and with an explosive temper and sharp elbows out, determined to take care of herself no matter the costs to anyone else.

I'm pretty certain she was physically punished as a child because, when her own temper goes, she whacks me with a hairbrush or uses other weapons like a hard shoe or a big bar of soap to wash my dirty, swear-word uttering mouth out with.

When quizzed years later about certain parts of her childhood, the *Señora* looks away and clams up, shaking her head silently, lips pressed together too tightly to let any words slip out. There are things in her past she will never talk about. Ever.

I know from her and her younger brother Bud that back when they are kids their mother Phyllis almost daily reminds our mother that, as a mere female, she will never amount to anything in the world. Only Bud, the boy, will get anywhere and be someone. Gotta have a penis or forget about it.

And one thing Bud tells me is particularly disturbing about our mother's past.

When he is four or five and his sister just a few years older, sometimes people or family come to visit their house. When that happens, Phyllis makes her little girl, my mother, go into a closet and locks the door on her. She is only permitted to come out when the visitors are gone.

And the coast is clear.

When Bud asks why his sister has to stay hidden in the dark closet while relatives are visiting, Phyllis has a logical answer:

"Because your sister Dorothy is too ugly for company to have to see."

So, while as an adult, I realize some emotional damage is needed to complete the whole Señora picture, as a child in Torremolinos this is way over my little head.

So, why has she brought us here?

It's a question in Torremolinos I constantly find myself wrestling with, usually asked by some kid who stands there armed with a perfectly logical explanation for his or her presence in this foreign land. Things like:

"My Dad is over here with an oil company." Nope. Try again.

"He's in the military and works at one of the US bases in Spain." No cigar for us Johnsons on that one.

"My parents are with the US embassy." Nuh-uh.

"My parents are writing a book on Spain." Nope.

Or even that great instantly acceptable one: "We have Spanish relatives." Guess again, pal. There's not one single drop of Spanish blood in us.

All these and more are offered and easily accepted as perfectly logical explanations for being an American in Spain.

But as for us we sort of stand there hemming and hawing, staring at our feet, because we really don't have any earthly reason to be here at all. We can't think of one.

None whatsoever at least as it applies to us Johnson kids.

Over the years I concoct various explanations, trying them all out on various people. Here are those that seem to work the best:

"My mother's kind of a nut. So she just did this." (That one usually gets you either a quizzical or a sympathetic look).

"She's like that guy in the story "Don Quijote" who reads so many books about knights in armor he goes wacky and things he's one."

"In her case, she read one too many Hemingway books, lost her mind, and came over here looking for bullfighters and romantic adventure."

Or, the sociological, emerging women's rights one (works best when told to females after the 70's): "After escaping two marriages she realizes she doesn't want to have to answer to a man, and yet she doesn't want to be just another divorced lady raising kids in the US suburbs."

This one usually takes a while to sink in, after which the young lady it's told to usually says something like:

"Right on, your mother sounds really cool."

Or the darker ones: "She wanted to keep us away from our father because:

a) she felt he was an ordinary working stiff who would be a dulling, stultifying influence on us,

or b) she was sticking it to him for one reason or another.

I never actually say this one back then, but people who I talk to about all this later have suggested it to me.

When you consider she told or father, as she told us, we are just going to Spain for a summer vacation, then whisks us away from him and his court approved rights to spend time with his own kids, it kind of makes sense.

In Torremolinos, ask the *Señora* why we have to live here in self-imposed exile and she just carefully examines her sharp fingernails, smiles, and explains it simply.

"We're staying here because we like it better here, don't we?"

What's so clever about that answer is that it throws any blame in the matter right back at our feet.

She has actually brought us to Spain because we ourselves her kids really wanted it that way. Not her, oh Lordy no, no way.

So she had no choice really, simply had to do it. Forced to by our impetuous childish commands.

Erase that last one, ball the others together, and you probably have a better explanation than you'll ever get from the *Señora*.

Or just amend the last one to read, "Because I, the *Señora*, like it better here."

Whatever the *Señora* wants us to do, that's what we do. That's why she's *"La Senora"*.

And we're not.

Sometimes, as a true lady should do, she attempts to cram a little culture into her unappreciative bratlings.

On car trips, in our chugging pale green VW bug, we mockingly refer to this, with phony English toffee-nose accents, as visits to yet one more "Romanesque church."

"Oh, we simply must stop here," La Mimi will say.

"Indeed," I opine, "You do of course realize that the church in this town is, dare I say:"

"Romanesque," El Miko explains.

Then we all laugh hysterically at the expense of the fuming *Señora*, who just wants us to enjoy what's there for Chrissakes.

Other times we're happier about where she takes in our little VW. Like down the coast to Gibraltar. That's an excursion we need no encouraging to take, despite the twisting coastal roads that make Mimi so carsick we have to stop often while she heaves by the roadside.

Partly, we like to go there because Gibraltar is at least somehow closer to the America we miss so much. As a British Overseas Territory, they actually speak English there, though the accent is kind of odd and they put "petrol" in their "lorries" which they park in a "gay-raj" and other strange things. It's still English so it feels more like home than Spain does.

In this British outpost, they also have marvelously tasty things we kids are used to finding in America that are lacking in Torremolinos. Like real creamy pasteurized milk you can drink without having to boil. Soft sugary cookies unlike the dry and cracker-like Spanish *Galletas María*. Rich milk chocolate bars from Cadbury's. Creamy English butter and luscious ice creams. Robertson's All Fruit Jam and, from a bakery on the main street, soft and sweet jelly donuts that melt in your mouth.

Yes! We need no prodding to head to the car when Gibraltar is mentioned, practically salivating like Pavlov's dogs.

We find it strange that to enter this little 2.3 square mile area you have to drive across the middle of an active airport runway. And that passports are required at a border crossing with stern-looking guards.

At this period, ordinary Spaniards are forbidden to enter without work permits, only foreigners like us.

Spain is pissed that Britain occupies this territory on what is an actual piece of the Iberian peninsula. England is given it in perpetuity by the Dutch in the 1713 Treaty of Utrecht. But Franco feels "treaty-schmeaty", this should be by all rights Spain.

Franco actually closes the border in 1969, sealing Gibraltar off from mainland Spain, and it doesn't reopen until 1982.

The towering rock of Gibraltar has for centuries been of strategic importance as it commands the very narrow entrance from the Atlantic to the Mediterranean sea. Across the strait of Gibraltar you can plainly see Morocco from high up on the massive nearly 1400 foot rock.

When you go up there to look, watch out for the Barbary Apes. The only wild apes or monkeys in all of Europe, they climb on your back and take any food you are holding or steal your camera and other possessions. They are big, the size of small chimpanzees, and it is rumored they bite.

Local legend has it that if the apes ever leave Gibraltar, the English will too. Hasn't happened yet.

During World War II, as a big British Naval base, Gibraltar was of great strategic importance. With Britain's navy there, it made it hard for German ships, especially submarines, to slip in and out of the Mediterranean undetected.

So Hitler prepared a secret plan, called Operation Felix, to attack Gibraltar with German troops and dislodge the British for good.

But one man stood in his way: Franco.

The wily dictator refused to allow any German soldiers on Spanish soil, which was a key part of the plan. So Operation Felix died on the operating table and Gibraltar stayed with the British crown.

While we kids happily go there for the goodies, our mother has another purpose: money changing. On the main street there's an Indian merchant who has a store selling cameras, rugs and other trinkets.

He also under the table gives a far better rate of exchange of pesetas for dollars than can be officially had in Spain.

So, while we kids happily return from Gibraltar stuffing our little faces, our mother is stuffing her bulging wallet with even more pesetas converted from our child support dollars to spend on her good times.

And she has a ball with that money. For one, she doesn't have to work at a job or even do a lick of dirty housework. She pays the "girl' a small fee to take care of the latter.

She has child support for us from my father and Spain is dirt cheap to live in. I think we pay 400 pesetas, about $12, for a maid to live with us and work full time for a month.

She's also single, relatively young (in her late 30's), and attractive: a slim brunette with green eyes and a good sense of humor. She catches the eye of plenty of men who come swarming around.

So, while there aren't hordes of bullfighters knocking on our door, there is this one retired *rejoneador,* or horseback bullfighter, who's around for a brief period. That's pretty exotic; a guy who actually fought bulls for a living, even if he did it from the relative safety of a galloping horse.

And there are enough chances at adventurous romance to satisfy any of her more Hemingwayesque aspirations.

As a kid you kind of notice this stuff with mild curiosity which only turns to alarm if any guy begins to draw at all close to any possibility of real Daddy stuff.

They all pretend they want to be your good buddy. But you instinctively know they're after what your mother has.

Usually, it's an annoyance, not a threat.

You just shrug it off as a grownups game of little interest to a child. But I actually notice a few of the men who sniff their way by like hound dogs on the scent of a tender female rabbit.

There are a number of married Spanish men who must thank their Catholic god for the presence in Spain of pretty *extranjeras*.

This gives them a chance to play around outside the narrow confines of Spanish society where they might otherwise get caught at an indiscretion.

They also don't need to pay for a *"puta"*, which is what the local ladies surely think our mother is. We threejg are likely seen by the villagers as "that American whore's kids."

Thanks to all the loose foreign ladies like our mother the Spanish men can dally and still return to their wives-for-life under the grace of the Father, the Son and the Holy Spirit, and the Pope in Rome.

It's sort of like the Heavenly Father created a separate play area where the strict rules of the church don't apply, so long-suffering Spanish men can escape the rigid confines of Catholic life.

And get a little tail.

One of these men is a magazine publisher we'll just call Fernando.

According to my mother he's trapped in a loveless marriage (I bet all the guys use that handy one) and just wants to have some fun.

He's decent enough, with a deep *macho* voice, brilliantined hair slicked straight back and shiny, a moustache and a friendly handshake, usually well-dressed with a sports jacket, matching kerchief and tie.

Kind of like a Spanish version of the film star David Niven

I hear that one day he's going to take us to his *finca*, or farm, in the country, where there will be horses to ride and a pool to swim in.

But somehow we never go there.

Then there's a South African guy who's a race car driver. I'm impressed by all his racing stories but notice he's a bit of a drinker.

And I really go off him when one day, influenced by more than a little *vino tinto*, he insists on taking a plastic jet I'm building, cramming a small Jetex motor that doesn't fit in it, and trying to make it fly.

I know enough about these things to be certain it won't work, but he won't listen, bullies on, and drunkenly hurls my smoking jet into the air, managing to break it into several pieces when it comes smashing back down on the street.

I'm not sure whether I'm more pissed off about his breaking the jet or just the fact that he's an aeronautical ignoramus, because that stuff counts big time in my book.

Either way, race car driver or not, I'm glad when he's history.

And, of course, there's Beardsley.

That's not exactly his name. He's a big, burly and hairy South African artist with a huge curly beard. His name is sort of like (I'm being discreet here) Herbert Sluttsley, which is bad enough, but we eventually dub him with a worse moniker: "Beardsley."

Remember, here in Torremolinos, everybody gets a nickname.

Sluttsley has a wife and kids and he's pretty poor so they live right in the *Carihuela* fishing village with the local fisherfolk. His kids run barefoot with the fishermen's kids, his wife stays put, and I guess Herbert runs around where he pleases.

"This is Herbert Sluttsely, kids. He's a painter. He's going to teach me how to speak Spanish."

That's how my mother introduces him to us, on the sunny porch of our rented villa.

It sort of makes sense; he needs money to buy paints, and she wants to learn the language, though why learn Spanish from a South African painter when the place is crawling with real Spaniards I'm not sure.

A few days later, when I wake up late from an afternoon nap, after El Miko and La Mimi have left, I innocently walk out on our large sunny porch and I discover that Sluttsley is teaching the *Señora* a lot more than just Spanish.

Though I guess you do have to use your tongue to speak it properly.

When I tell my brother and sister about this, we agree this is not a positive development. And we dub this hairy invader to our home as "Beardsley".

No matter, the Senora begins to try to push both "Beardsley" and the barefoot "Beardsley" kids on us.

She even forces me to invite his scrawny older son to my birthday party, where he sings a beautiful Spanish fishing village flamenco birthday song to me and I scowl cruely at him all the while.

It's not his fault, he's probably a great kid. He's just got the wrong dad, that's all, so go away Beardsley brat.

No matter how we howl and whine about this dreadful bearded interloper, we just can't seem to shake the man.

Somehow the Señora and we kids end up in a hotel in Madrid at some point, with my mother explaining to us that Sluttsley says he's about ready to leave his wife and we will soon all go live with him in Zaragoza in some wretched artist's garret: her vision of romantic paradise, our deepest Hell.

She's just waiting for him to go dump wifey and call for The Señora to come sweeping into his hairy arms. In the meantime she goes out that evening in Madrid with an American girl friend, leaving us to entertain ourselves in the hotel room with art pads and crayons, no doubt like budding artistic little Sluttsleys in training.

When our mother returns late that night, our artwork is waiting for her. Every wallpapered wall in the hotel room has been decorated with the same bold, artistic statement:

"WE HATE BEARDSLEY!"

Whether that protest is the end of him or, much more likely, he never actually really means to leave his wife and consequently never calls, that is all she wrote.

Beard boy is history.

If you ask me, whether you want to call him Beardsley or his real name, it is the latter truth: he never means to leave his wife and kids, he's just looking for a piece of ass.

Kids can sense what's real and what's not.

Sluttsley is shit.

Still, all in all, you've got to give my mother credit for having the chutzpah to want to go out and have some romance and fun in her life, to escape the drab drone of everyday suburbia and reach for something more.

And she manages to pull the sort of Hemingway dream stuff off damn well.

I mean, how many women can say before they die they've had boyfriends who were newspaper publishers, dashing Grand Prix race car drivers from South Africa, Spanish bullfighters, and romantic starving artists from Australia?

Think about it. You're only here for a short time and then you're cold and dead for a hell of a lot longer. So, as they say in Spain, take advantage:

"*Aproveche.*"

And our mother *"aproveches"* everything she can get her hands on.

As far as her children possibly getting screwed out of so much in the bargain, I doubt this enters her mind at all.

Like so many of the other ex-pat parents, she can easily dismiss such nonsense ideas with any number of ready-made platitudes:

"These are such lucky kids, they are actually experiencing another culture."

Perhaps one day someone may be able to explain to me what the actual advantage is of "experiencing another culture." To this day, I have yet to discover it.

When I finally get to return to my own country I realize there are so many other cultures to experience already here in America. The USA is a rich tapestry of many different nations, no need to look for any in foreign lands. They are already here.

"Our children are being broadened by living abroad."

Gee. If so, I was "broadened" for years. Can't say it did me a whit of good. Reading books on my own did a much better job of widening my world.

"We are actually doing them a huge favor by making the hard sacrifices of living over here."

Oh yeah, guys. My heart weeps for you. Have another glass of *vino tinto* to console yourselves.

Besides my mother feels entitled to do whatever she wants to.

We are, after all, just the kids.

She's the *Señora*.

.

8
Los Aviones

IT'S EARLY ON THE MORNING of our second summer in Torremolinos and everybody's still asleep. A salty, cool Mediterranean breeze blows through the window, ruffling the white curtains. My brother Mark lies in his bed across the room dreaming, probably about the young girl who works at the cobblers and has caught his eye.

Me, I sit up bolt upright in the bed. Something has awakened me.

It's like a noise you feel but can't actually hear, like the deep hum and throb of a powerful engine somewhere hidden below decks on a huge boat. It wakes me up and calls to me.

I pull on my shorts and T-shirt and pad out of the house behind the church, walking bare foot down the cool blue grey stone road to the lookout by the old tower on top of the cliff.

I reach the railing and rest my arms on cold green wrought iron to look out over the sea and the sleeping Bahondillo fishing village below. In the distance I can hear the sound of small waves breaking over the yellow sand and a dog barking.

Suddenly , a sleek silver blur shoots by, howling like a banshee at over 300 miles per hour.

It's a gleaming metal Messerschmidt, a true ME-109, streaking by like a bullet with a high pitched whine of 26 whirling cylinders, all 1,610 horsepower, at full crank.

Yeah, man. This, for me, is heaven.

For you see I am in love...entranced with anything that flies: birds, kites, skyrockets, paper airplanes, and of course real airplanes, "*los aviones,*" especially the kind in the World War II movies and books I grew up with back in Chevy Chase.

And, guess what. Back then Spain has a lock on an unusual corner of that part of heaven: the Nazi side.

The WWII airplanes from the bad guys.

All that German stuff you only see in movies where the brave RAF pilots are scrambling to knock it out of the search-lit skies over London, the aircraft that strafed our LST landing craft on the beaches of Normandy, the bombers that Rommel launched against the allies in the hot sands of North Africa, all that stuff you'd never ever see for real in America: it's around in Torremolinos.

And, it's not in some dusty museum sitting idly on its tail wheels, it's in the sky everyday.

Because the Spanish Air Force is still flying it at the time I'm there. And, when they crash one, the Spanish CASA aircraft factory turns out a replacement.

It's like a flying reminder of the deal Franco cut with the Germans to help him win the Civil War. The Krauts send him all manner of aircraft; in fact they use Spain as a sort of laboratory to test their aircraft in.

What better way to learn which bombs and bullets kill people best than to try them out on real human test subjects: the Spaniards. Ever see Picasso's painting of the flames and bombs and anguish of "Guernica"? That is only a Kraut test for WWII.

Then, after the Falangists use their German built aircraft to win in Spain and somehow, after the crafty old Generalisimo weasels out of having to help Germany fight the big one, Spain keeps the technology and goes right on building and flying Messerschmidts and Heinkels and Junkers and Bukkers and so on.

Come to think of it, who's going to come after them for patent infringement? Goering? Himmler? Der Fuhrer himself? Anybody who matters is dead or in Argentina or actually hiding in Spain.

But this is all history and the only part that really matters to me is the one whizzing by in the skies above the beach and the town. At the sound of a throbbing aircraft engine I drop whatever I am doing and rush to the window or any vantage point to see what is about to fly by.

And I am rewarded again and again with sights no ordinary American boy could ever hope to see.

Like the Messerschmidt I see from the tower that morning. After World War II, Spanish factories put nearly 250 of them into the skies of España, calling them, not ME-109s, but HA-1109s.

Whatever number you want to call it, it's still a bonifide Messerschmidt.

And sooner or later you're bound to see one blow by like a Nazi bat screaming out of whatever hell der Fuhrer is roasting in.

What a thrill to see up close the deadly German fighter that made the guys flying Spitfires and Hurricanes, and especially the crews of lumbering B-19 bombers, nearly pee in their pants with fear.

Or, like the squadron of twin-engine, bubble nosed Heinkel 111's based in Málaga. They roar overhead on a daily basis, twin 1350 horsepower engines whining with a deafening high-pitched sound. They're our most visible, and very audible, local air force. And, except for the missing Nazi emblems, they could be roaring out of Der Fuhrer's Germany.

In 1958, I watch the Heinkels wing off to quell an Arab rebellion in Spain's African colony of Ifni, known then as the Spanish Sahara, on the West Coast of Africa, just south of Morocco.

Spain has held the Italy-sized territory since 1936 and sees it as a buffer for its Canary Island possession 200 miles further west out in the Atlantic.

But now the Sawahari desert tribes who live there want independence, just like their neighbor to the North, Morocco, recently won its freedom from the French with Sawahari help.

In a strange twist of fate, these Arab tribesmen are the descendants of the same Arabs who colonized and ruled Spain until Queen Isabel and King Ferdinand chased the last of them out in 1492.

Now the Spaniards rule them.

What goes around, comes around

The desert tribesmen have been promised that Morocco will return the favor of the help they gave, and will fight with The Sawaharis against Spain. The bombers from Málaga are part of what Franco sends to put them both down.

The fact that Morocco never comes to help and actually cuts off the Sawahari's supplies and munitions at the crucial moment probably hurts almost as much as the 500 lb. bombs the Heinkels rain down.

In the age of jets and atomic weapons, the image of burnoose clad Arabs on horseback and camel facing off against Nazi-era bombers seems very surreal. So does the roaring formation that the bombers fly low over Torremolinos, buzzing deafeningly by one after another as they wing their way to the desert war.

Not too many years earlier if you'd seen that sight in London, they would have been dropping bombs on you as Walter Winchell broadcast to the world from a hotel rooftop.

I can still hear the whining roar of one He-111 buzzing the Plaza Central on its return, the grinning pilots and bombardier-front gunner visible in the clear glass nose canopy as they headed for home and a glass of *Malaga Dulce*.

There's also the twhock-thwock-thwocketa of the three-engines powering the Junkers 52, a corrugated tin, flying museum piece. If you've ever seen historical shots of the Ford Tri-Motor, think about something on those lines, painted dull air force olive green, big fixed wheels hanging down, throbbing it's way slowly over the blue Mediterranean sky, like some kind of Spanish/German tin goose.

This slow lumbering bird is sort of the German side's version of America's cargo workhorse, the twin-engine Douglas DC-3, known as the Dakota. For the Allies, fleets of DC-3's ferried supplies and troops everywhere, and on D-Day masses of paratroopers jumped over Normandy from Dakotas.

The Junkers 52 was the Dakota of the Dark Side.

Junkers flew Hitler's troops and/or parachuted them into places like Poland, France and Denmark and was a vital strategic tool used in the invasions of Crete and Africa.

Before that, they played a key role for Spain's Generalisimo Franco. As a Spanish general in command of the Army of Africa, he joined a fascist military coup against the nascent, democratically elected Republic and desperately needed to get his army across the straits of Gibraltar to Spain. But with warships blocking the way and few aircraft in Franco's possession, the Republicans held him in check.

A quick secret deal with Adolf Hitler suddenly got him a fleet of 20 troop-carrying JU-52s and German pilots to wing his army, and his cause, to mainland Spain.

The rest, as they say, is history.

Now, in the skies above Torremolinos, these museum pieces are flying for my personal delight in 1958, and will be in fact, till 1974.

Then there is the Spanish Independence Day that the head of the Spanish Air Force primary flying school in Granada decides to stage a coastal air parade using his fleet of two-seater Bukker biplanes.

While the Generalísimo in Madrid is reviewing a fly by of Spain's latest jet-fighters courtesy of the USA, we are treated to something that looks like it goes all the way back, not just to World War II, but to the Great War itself and to movies like "The Blue Max" and "Wings".

Imagine the sky buzzing with the hum of small radial engines as about fifty biplanes slowly rise and fall in formation and two peel off to swoop and dive bomb the beach, then return to a pack that would have looked good flying over the trenches at Verdun in 1916.

Have I told you that to me this is heaven? It thrills me just to put these words down on the page.

Back then there is also a nastier, *Americano* superiority side to my seeing all of this. Whenever I think about the Spanish Air Force flying old Nazi equipment, I inevitably pat America and my team on the back for flying the most modern jets ever invented.

The good old USAF isn't flying a bunch of prop-driven, World War II museum-quality, equipment from the losing side. No sir, they are rocketing around in supersonic F-100 Super Sabres or even the sleek F-104 Starfighters that actually look like space rockets with tiny wings.

Clearly the Spaniards are living in some past era while the great Americans are rocketing boldly into the shiny bright future, a future that I assure myself will include me.

The first winter we are in Torremolinos, this smug, satisfied feeling of superiority gets appropriately put in its place, beginning one night at the Cine Universal. Before the feature film comes on, the inevitable NoDo newsreel temporarily leaves news of *Generalisimo Franco* and his many glorious accomplishments. Instead the Spanish newsreel focuses on the new American space program and its hapless struggle to launch some sort of thing into space.

As I watch in dismay, several rockets lift off the pad at Cape Canaveral (Kennedy these days), only to veer drunkenly from their trajectories and explode helplessly in hot yellow and orange fireballs, then plunge slowly to the ground, further exploding into blazing white hot smithereens.

What's worse, the entire Spanish audience howls with delighted laughter at the embarrassing sight. How can they? It's humiliating. The great United States, scientific leader of the world, held up as a laughingstock in front of a nation whose pilots fly around in WWII antiques. I cringe in my seat.

But the worst is yet to come.

One evening in November, some Spanish kids I'm hanging with take me to the lookout by the old watchtower. They check their watches and scan the clear winter night skies. At exactly 10:03 p.m. someone spots it and points it out with an excited shout.

"Allí, mira! El Spootnik!!"

There it is, way up in the heavens where the helplessly exploding American rockets can't even dream to reach. Against the dark black of the Spanish winter night, one of the bright pinpoints of stars is moving silently across the sea of space. It's sending the world a message from Russia, with or without love: "I am the Sputnik II satellite, behold my Soviet glory in the cold black void of outer space!"

There for the whole entire world to see, the Russians' second successful satellite rubs in the global triumph of Sputnik I, this time putting a living creature into space.

Somewhere up there in that shiny, moving pinpoint of light, is a little stray dog picked up from the streets of Moscow named Laika. She must have initially thanked her lucky stars that people took her in and cared for her and fed and petted her. She surely felt she had found Doggie Heaven.

Now little Laika probably wonders where everyone went and when the people will come back to feed her again. Soon, equipment failure and an overheating capsule will end her life out in the stars, a short existence that proved to be not so lucky or heavenly after all.

Down on Planet Earth, in a place called Torremolinos, I wonder what has happened to the once great U. S. of A. I try to rationalize it and shrug it off.

It's not like it's about people piloting real aircraft, it's just about sending bits of tin and little dogs into space. I try to re-focus on the flying stuff around, and stifle the idea that the US may not be as wonderful as it thinks it is.

Besides there's a great air show going on all around me every day.

By the way, there is some non-Nazi equipment as well. I also am thrilled to see the AT-6 Texan trainers Spain got from the Americans that you now see today in the U.S. whenever you look way up to see some humming specks in the sky write short advertising slogans in puffs of white smoke.

There are a few Lockheed Shooting Star jets, here and there and F-86 Sabres.

And, of course, civilian aircraft. The twin prop Convair that flies daily to Madrid and that nightly sweeps the village with its landing lights at ten p.m. as it lowers for its return. The light planes that fly in and out, including the gull-winged Jodel the German guy who lives in front of the church tools around in, buzzing the old watchtower as he does. The flying school biplanes that would stunt over the village, looping and rolling as I watch in awe, reciting with my Spanish friends the maneuvers they make.

"A loop and a roll."

" An Immelman."

"A barrel roll and an inverted loop."

"A hammerhead stall." And so on.

Like I said, back then I am in love with things that fly. To this day, I still am fascinated by any old airport and everything there. But with time, I better understand the reason behind this fixation.

It is really all about my father. And his absence.

Planes are my only connection to him for over ten years, except for a brief visit home for a month or so. I never see him for so incredibly long but I miss him greatly. I know he works in the aviation business, started his career in it with some long gone outfit called Pickwick Airways out on the West Coast.

So, my dad loves planes, I love planes.

It makes me feel closer to my father so far away, with every aircraft that flies by, somehow I feel it makes a bond between us that our infrequent letters and Xmas gifts from 5,000 miles away never can.

Once or twice I hear his distant voice when our mother takes us over to the Post and Telephone office on the main carretera. There, with an appointment, she can arrange for an overseas call, something we couldn't do at home in Spain in those days even if we had a phone. And, of course, there is no internet.

So, one by one, our mother brings me and Mark and Mimi into the phone cubicle and shuts the door, so each of us can talk to dad while she stays, listens in, and tell us what top say.

It feels so good to hear his voice and try to cling to our fading memories of him and our life in an America that is starting to drift into the misty distance.

Listening there beside me, with a firm hand on my shoulder, my mother keeps prompting things she thinks I should say.

"Tell him how much you love swimming at the beach!"

"Say that you're really looking forward to going to see Morocco!"

"Tell him there's a good local school you'll be going to and learn to speak Spanish!"

This three-sided conversation goes on this way until it's time for my brother or sister to get their turn to be told exactly what to say to dad.

"I love you, son."   "I love you, dad."

And then he is gone.

And the only place I feel I can really touch him is when I see some machine flying through the blue Spanish sky. It's a plane and it's all about my father. At least in my mind.

Maybe ultimately I sense this when I get older and closer to choosing a career, that this love of planes has to do with missing my father and not necessarily about who I really am. Probably so.

Because I remember during my college years sitting in my itchy blue grey Air Force ROTC uniform in a room in an Air Force hospital in Oklahoma. My pupils are wildly dilated by some drop of clear liquid, and I feel a twinge in my left eye as a flight surgeon looks in with a flashlight and says in his MidWest accent:

"Son, looks like yew don't have thuh best night vision in yer left ah."

I find myself unqualified to further pursue my course to become an Air Force fighter pilot. And I remember being strangely somewhat relieved and not very crushed. Not because I won't be trained to possibly fly against the North

Vietnamese and maybe even bomb them. I just wasn't that politically conscious. Yet.

I am relieved I won't have to sign the next seven years of my life to the Air Force, two of them in college ROTC and five in actual service. I feel I don't even know who I am at that very moment and am in no way prepared to commit to one direction for most of the next decade.

So there in the Oklahoma hospital I don't feel I've lost that much.

So, I won't fly. So what.

That, of course, isn't how I feel in Torremolinos. Then, flying fighter jets for the USAF is an ultimate fantasy, one made all the cooler one summer morning by a surprise event.

"The Attack of the F-100's."

It happens like this. We are living in the *Bahondillo*, down below the cliffs, in a small apartment complex. I am out in the garden with my friend Dana when there is a deafening thunderclap from the sky.

We look up to see a gleaming silver American F-100 fighter jet roar by low, headed towards Málaga.

Then we nearly get knocked right over by yet another thunderclap as a second F-100 streaks by from the other direction. Instantly both jets turned out towards the sea, wheel around and head right towards us in tight formation maybe a hundred feet or less over the small waves.

Just before they crash into the cliffs behind us, they pull up slightly and buzz the town above. A few seconds later they come roaring back around the cliffs to make another pass with their ear-splitting scream.

Up above the center of town, in the main market place, pandemonium sets in. My mother is there quietly perusing the stalls of vegetables and fresh fish when the jets roar right over head with a deafening blast.

Maybe it's because memories of the Spanish Civil war are still fresh, maybe it's just the Spanish propensity to believe that the worst can happen, the people became convinced war has broken out.

They run frantically, knocking over stalls of produce and hiding under cars shouting it's war: *"La guerra! La guerra!"* as the screaming F-100's streak back again and again.

How are they to know it wasn't really war, just some jet jockeys from Rota air base trying to impress some pretty girls they'd met in the bars in Torremolinos.

Down below I am so totally in seventh heaven, my excitement growing with every pass the silver fighters make. It's our own private air show, from the greatest air force in the world. Ours. No second-hand Nazi equipment for our boys.

The final act is awesome.

Coming from opposite ends of the village, the jets streak close together low over the *Bahondillo* fishing village then loop up in opposite directions, right over my head, arcing straight up, then over on to their backs and back down again to complete the bottom of the loop less than a hundred feet over some fields of sugar cane.

And to really finish with a bang, they kick on their afterburners, yellow flames shooting out their tailpipes as they accelerate in opposite directions breaking the sound barrier and rattling windows as they zoom off with two resounding booms that shake your very bones.

As they vanish into the clear blue sky and their rumbling recedes, I hear the sugar cane in the fields cracking and snapping from the wind the jets generated on their last pass, it was that low.

And, at least at the time, long before Oklahoma and eye doctors, I know what I want to work with for a living.

"Los aviones".

David M. Johnson

9

Romeria

I LOOK LIKE A DORK. I feel like a dork.

In fact, I am a dork, at least for as long as I have to wear this totally dumbass costume.

I have on grey pants with a red cummerbund-like sash hastily made out of some spare cloth, a white shirt open at the collar, and a dopey cheap paper version of those Andalusian *señoritos* grey flat brimmed kind of hats that the guy Spanish dancers sometimes wear.

My mother says I have to look this way because of the *romería*, a springtime country fiesta the village is holding up in the mountains.

But, as for me and my brother, who is suffering the mortal indignity of the same ridiculous getup, we know who the real culprit is: mom, once again inflicting her meddlesome visions of how things could look in her dreams versus our actual real lives.

Oblivious to our unwillingness to go along with yet another of her embarrassing, at least to us, schemes, she always smiles and says the same kind of "1984," "war is peace" kind of doubletalk.

"But you really <u>want</u> to dress up like little Spanish *señoritos*. After all, it's the *romería*!"

Yeah, mom. just like we really <u>wanted</u> to stay in Spain and not return to our home in the States and the life we knew and really <u>wanted</u> to not be able to see our dad ever again. Maybe next we'll really <u>want</u> to jump off the cliff into the sea and drown!

You tell us, lady. You seem to have all the answers.

Besides we're not little Spanish *señores* or *señoritos*. We're 100% bonafide USA Americans forced, for the moment, to dress up in cheap paper hats and wear clumsy red cloth cummerbunds around our waists like some kind of cut-rate 5 and 10 cent parody of real Spaniards, whatever the heck they may be.

This is just so wrong. I'm supposed to be back in America dressed for school or in my cub scout uniform or suited up for the 1950s version of Pee Wee football, and not in some weird planet called "Spain" dressed up like somebody's cheap vision of a Spaniard.

Really mom.

It makes no difference; we're trapped looking like two prize idiots, at least for a while. Scowling, we pose for some stupid pictures with our sister Mimi who's all done up like a Spanish flamenco dancer, right down to the mantilla in her hair and real lipstick and all.

But she's a girl, she probably likes dress up, that's what girls are supposed to do, isn't it?

Besides, she's been taking flamenco lessons with her girlfriends in a room above one of the local bars near the Plaza Central, stamping and clicking their castanets away, whirling around to tunes with names like *"La Sevillana"* and *"La Malagueña"*, trying to look fierce and proud and Spanish, which is no mean feat for a ten-year-old blonde from Chevy Chase, Maryland.

With their teacher they're even going to perform at the *romería*, a sight sure to warm our beaming mother's heart.

"My little Spanish *señorita!!*"

As for me and Mark, we could puke and die. After the photo, we'd like to run and hide, but instead we're forced to walk up the Calle San Miguel in our clownish faux Spaniard costumes, past all the laughing village kids we know.

And then, worst of all, along with some of our similarly tortured-by-clothes American friends, we have to climb up into a mule cart that's been festooned with flowers and ribbons, and then paraded through the village up high for all to see, sort of like the way prisoners about to be hanged used to be displayed to the taunting crowds on their way to the gallows.

The local kids yell at us and laugh at our ridiculous getups. No way are their mommas dressing them like clowns.

Then the cart, part of a large procession of similar conveyances plus people on horse and mule back, makes its way up above the town, past the *Calvario* village, and heads towards the foot of the mountains that rise high above Torremolinos.

We make our way past small farms and tall fields of sugar cane, along dusty country roads that wind slowly upwards.

As soon as we realize our mom, taking some other route to the festivities, is nowhere to be seen, our odious hats go sailing high above the stalks of sugar cane and the cummerbunds get jettisoned into irrigation ditches by the side of the road.

Ah, now that's better.

What? Those hats? Uh, gee, mom, we lost them. Maybe some Spanish kids took them. Yeah, that's it, they probably really <u>wanted</u> to wear them so they could look like a bunch of idiots dressed by their mommas.

Right at the foot of the tallest mountain behind town, there's a cluster of farm buildings and tall trees around a large concrete reservoir about the size of a football field. I know the place because I've been there with local friends catching fish and eels that wriggle and slither like crazy when you haul them out.

This is where the fresh water that pours out of the fountains in town comes from (maybe the eels give it that special taste). And it's where the *romería* is to be held.

That part's okay, especially once we've ditched the sartorial stupidity.

There are lots of people from the village and a crowd of *extranjeros* like us as well. There's music from a phonograph set up under the trees with some cheap speakers strung about, and further down towards the other end some guys are playing flamenco guitar under the trees. There are kids playing soccer and other games, like a Spanish version of tag that we join in on.

There's sangria and wine for the grownups and sodas for the kids (some kids choose the wine or sangria anyway), including real honest to god Coca Cola, for us one of the few signs of real civilization in *España*.

If only these heathens had more of life's essentials like maybe Skippy Peanut Butter and hamburgers and Campbell's Cream of Mushroom soup and toilet paper that was actually soft.

But that's another matter. Today, like it or not, we are doing the *romería.*

And it's worth doing, though it's a blazing hot day. We play some games, eat steaming chicken, rice and seafood *paella*, made in huge pans over open fires, and *tortillas*, not like the Mexican kind, but made instead with egg, potato and onion, like what the Italians call *frittata.*

We also down as many Cokes as we are allowed and, thoroughly sated, squeeze in a little siesta in the shade of a large tree.

Then it's time for the flamenco show starring my sister and her little friends, all led by their teacher, whose substantial plumpness stretches tight the red polka dots on her flamenco dancing dress.

A scratchy 45 rpm record, warbling a bit from the uneven turntable, bleats out a *Sevillana.* The young girls take their places, assume dance poses and, on a signal from the teacher, launch into the flamenco thing, or at least their version of it.

They gamely strut and whirl and stamp about a makeshift plywood stage under the elm trees, clicking their castanets raggedly at the appropriate points, stamping their little red-heeled shoes and making the fiercest faces possible.

You see the flamenco we've seen isn't like the kind of dancing back in America where girls are told to plant a constant beaming smile on their faces, no matter what they are doing, like the way they do a split and then smile to show it was easy, which of course it isn't.

No. In flamenco, it seems to us, they'd throw you out for that. Instead, in all the shows we've seen people have this stern, serious, fierce look on their face, sort of like they were in pain and were majorly pissed off about it and determined not to let anyone see it.

So smiling is a general no-no. Sure, they must smile sometimes, but that's how it looks to me.

Anyhow, the little flamenco show's pretty good considering, probably about the level of any grade school music recital where the violins aren't quite in tune but you can make out the song enough to figure out what they really intended to do if they only actually could.

The dancing certainly delights the large crowd of all the beaming foreign parents and their friends, and the small group of villagers who look on with some amusement.

Think about it. What if a bunch of Turks started living in say Tulsa, Oklahoma. And come the rodeo and county fair time, the little Turkish kids dressed up as cowboys and cowgirls and did a little square dance routine.

It'd be kinda cute. I guess.

After Mimi's third or fourth flamenco dance I kind of lose interest and my mind drifts 3,000 miles away to America and visions of football practice and home and dad and all the things that are beginning to sound as far away and muted as that tinny warbling music from the beat up record player. I try to hang onto to my previous life, though it seems to be fading like a dog-eared old photograph.

I wander over to the other side of the reservoir where a crowd is gathered under some cypress trees and this arouses my curiosity.

As I draw nearer, the tinny sound of the Sevillanas coming from the dance recital record player and the sound of small American feet fiercely stomping on plywood fades. It gives way to this growing rhythmic pounding coming from the cypress tree area I'm headed for.

My longing for America momentarily blows away on the warm mountain breeze as the rhythm grows louder and I come closer to it.

It's sort of like a heart beat with one super strong pulse.

TAK! takatak! TAK! takatak! TAK! takatak! TAK! takatak!

This hypnotic beat gets louder and louder as it pulls me into the crowd and I realize where it's coming from them, they are clapping in unison, or pounding on tables as they gaze smiling, faces beaming with joy, to the center of the gathering.

There, in a shaft of sunlight on top of a simple wood table, is a dark-skinned village girl, several years older than me, maybe 15. I recognize her from the *Bahondillo* fishing village.

She's dancing flamenco, the real deal, moving slowly to the beat, her hands and arms undulating and intertwining like beautiful tan serpents in the most unbelievably graceful style I have ever seen.

They look like they are telling ancient stories to the TAK! Takatak! of the beat.

She isn't wearing a pretty store bought flamenco dress with polka dots or have on fancy red shoes. In fact, she isn't wearing shoes at all, she's barefoot and has on the same simple dress I have seen her sport around the village.

And the people in the crowd aren't dolled up in *típico* Spanish *señorito* costumes, paper or otherwise. They're dressed like the common, poor villagers they are.

But what's going on has a grace and a beauty and a pure, unbridled joy that money can only dream of.

Up on the table, the girl turns her head this way, then that, a small rivulet of sweat rolling down her temple and brown cheek, and, as she takes her simple skirt in one hand, her hips slowly and naturally sway from side to side.

I am mesmerized.

I gaze into mysteries I had never in my life imagined. It's the first time I ever look at a woman and really saw her as a whole other creature from me.

It's like she is from another planet, or maybe I am, but either way you can see there's something really different going on. And it's good.

It's the first time I ever get the notion of sex, not the act, but the spirit, because she's dancing it and every other secret of life as well.

She smiles radiantly as her bare feet stamp to the rhythm, then she turns her head my way, smiling and caught up in the sheer joy of the dance.

And I look deep into the dark, sparkling eyes of Spain.

Torremolinos

David M. Johnson

10
Manolito

THEY SAY SOMETIMES GOOD THINGS just fall out of the sky. That's pretty much how I find my best friend our first long lonely winter in Torremolinos.

Soon after summer ends, *Los Johnsons* find ourselves living in a two-story house in front of the big whitewashed adobe church, a house with a high rooftop terrace. I spend a lot of my time up on the terrace on my own looking for any aircraft that might just cruise by or flying my own airborne contraption: a homemade kite I've pieced together from bamboo swiped from a nearby garden and newspaper, all stuck together with flour and water glue.

This isn't after all a time and place where you just stop in at Wal Mart or Toys R Us and pick up a kite. If you want a toy in Torremolinos, you've got to do-it-yourself.

Sure, my kite soars wildly up into the blue Spanish winter sky, so it's mildly interesting, but somehow it lacks the truly electrifying thrill of something that actually has wings and maybe even a pulsing, snarling engine.

I get bored.

So I put it away and go outside to take a stroll up Calle San Miguel. When I reach the corner I see something that stops me in my tracks: a group of Spanish kids follow an older, balding man in his forties who carries an immense model glider with a wingspan of at least two meters. It looks big enough to take a small child or one of the scruffy village dogs on a flight around the town.

Together they all march inside a building with official-looking gold and red seals and a red and yellow Spanish flag on it, in front of the church and down from our house. I've heard my mother say it's some kind of government building, something to do with Franco's political party, the *Falange*, and that they are "fascists" which is bad.

I don't care about "fascists" or any politics at that point, they could be Democrats or Republicans or Whigs for all it matters.

They've got an airplane.

Since I vaguely know one of the kids in the group, I tag along unobtrusively behind the little gang and peer around the corner into the big room they've gone into.

It's my true vision of paradise. From the ceiling, hang four or five finished model airplanes. All around the room, there are other miniature aircraft in varying states of completion, pinned to diagrammed plans, or clamped to the table as their glue hardens.

In one corner a couple of young Spaniards are steaming pine struts over a rusted tea kettle on an ancient electric burner, and bending them to make rounded wing tips. Everywhere there's the smell of fresh cut wood and doped up paper wings and model airplane glue. I like this.

No. I love this.

Somebody sees me peering around the corner and invites me in. Quickly realizing my Spanish is rather limited, this boy still patiently and slowly shows me all the aircraft and tells me what this group of boys is up to, repeating things until I get what he's saying.

He says his name is Manolito. His father is the smiling, baldish guy who runs the place. It's sort of like a Boy Scout group, only a group that's basically interested in learning about *aeromodelismo*, making model planes.

They get the materials and the room from the government party, the *falange*, but I get the idea this is all about making planes and not fascist salutes and goosesteps and pledges to defend Franco to the death.

Manolito's brother, Juanito, a handsome older kid of about sixteen is one of the guys steaming pine struts in the corner. That afternoon they are going to try out several of the newly made gliders of a particular model called a "Chimbo,"as well as the huge one his father brought in to repair.

Do I want to come and see?

Does *un oso* shit in *el bosque*? You bet the bear does.

That afternoon I'm there as the group leaves the *Falangista* party headquarters carrying four or five model airplanes, plus repair pieces, glue, and launching lines.

Buzzing with excitement we make our way through the center of town, picking up a crowd of curious kids as we go, and head up the slope of the hill to a dusty field above the Calvario right next to where the unhappy-looking bad boys *reformatorio* is located at the foot of the mountains.

As any English-speaking kids see us and ask what's going on, I'm proud to tell them all about it.

"We are going to fly these planes, tow them aloft and watch them soar through the skies!"

"We", I say to point out the fact that I now consider myself part of this particular group of young *falangistas* or, if you will, Franco Youth.

You know what, if I had to officially join somebody's fascist party to do all this, at this time in my life, when aircraft are like gods to me, I probably would have without question.

So sure, gimme the jackboots and the uniform, just as long as there are planes, I am there, pal, *Víva Franco!* or whatever you want.

Kids don't think much deeper than that. And that's probably how you put together a Hitler Youth in the first place. Fortunately this one's only about model airplanes and not the dark stuff.

I remember it isn't a great day for flying planes as there aren't any thermals to lift the gliders higher after they release from the tow lines a hundred feet or so above the huffing, puffing designated runner who scrambles to tow them aloft.

But I do distinctly recall the mesmerizing thrill of seeing a "Chimbo" slowly arc and wheel through the blue Spanish sky, like a thing of incomparable grace and sheer aerodynamic poetry, and looking over to share a smile with Manolito, knowing he is equally excited by the same vision.

We are fast friends from that day on, *amigos* that for each other just sort of dropped out of the clear, blue sky.

My new friend's full name is Manuel Salvador Murillo de Garcia y Henares.

But, as you might figure, just plain Manolito (or Little Manolo) works fine for most everybody. He's taller than me, a bit skinny or even gangly, and pretty dark-skinned like a real *Anadaluz* or even a *gitano* from the gypsy cave dwelling further down the cliff.

Besides just finding somebody my age that shares the same interests, I discover Manolito brings so many other cool things to the party.

Like his father, Juan. Besides being the nicest, warmest and most fun loving and unpretentious adult I know at this time, he's got something that makes him instantly cool with me.

He's in aviation just like my Dad. Only Juan's a pilot.

And, Juan isn't just any old pilot. He's a military pilot in the Spanish Air Force. Now that is the height of Spanish cool to me (setting aside the USAF modern jet thing), to be around military planes and air force bases all day. I stand in awe of that, though he doesn't actually have the best job in his outfit.

If I remember correctly, at the start of the Spanish civil war, Manolito's dad flew for the losing side. He piloted rapid snub-nosed Russian-made Polikarpov I-16 fighters called *Ratas*, or flying "rats" by the Natonalists and *Moscas* or "flies" by the Republicans flying them.

Whether he made the switch to Franco's side willingly or was captured and given the choice of fly or die, I am not clear about. But this checquered political past means that, at an age when he should have a superior rank, he has been passed over repeatedly and is still only a lieutenant colonel.

He is relegated to piloting the ancient, tin goose, tri-motored Junkers 52 transports that lumber slowly through the sky, clattering with a whumpeta-whump of three old radial engines, while other more politically correct pilots fly the modern aircraft and ascend the ranks.

No matter. He's still a bonfide pilot and in the military. That's good enough for me. Plus, he's the nicest, funniest guy you'd ever want to meet and, though I am not conscious of it at the time, the one real, no bullshit, father figure I find here in all my years so far away from my own dad.

Then, there's Manolito's mom, Maruja. A vivacious brunette from Almeria, she's always got a smile or a laugh and a hug. When I'm invited for lunch at their modest old second-story apartment in a worn, slightly crumbling, adobe building on the edge of town, she makes these scrumptious chicken *croquetas* I can taste to this day.

Manolitos older brother, Juanito ("Little Juan" to distinguish him from his father Big Juan), completes the family. Like Manolito, he's dark-skinned, but perhaps more handsome and, at sixteen, into the ladies, something me and his brother have yet to really become aware of. There's time for that.

For now, I've got a Spanish friend to hang with and explore the town on foot or on our bicycles, and to talk with about what it might be like to fly this plane or that one, maybe to have flown bravely in World War II and, if so, in what aircraft and for what side.

Like me, Manolito's head turns automatically at the slightest sound of a plane, and we rush together to the nearest vantage point to quickly spot and identify whatever it is that's flying in our vicinity.

I also learn more Spanish hanging with Manolito and other village kids than I would have from all the schools in Spain. As a kid, you just soak stuff like that up like a bone-dry sponge snarfs up water.

No formal Spanish lessons needed.

Much of the Spanish I learn hanging with Manolito is the local Southern dialect called *Andaluz* and spoken, naturally, by the Andalusians of southern Spain. Unlike the crisp, carefully enunciated *Castellano* I learn later in Madrid, *Andaluz* favors shortening words and entire phrases, kind of a lazy man's approach to the language.

So somebody in Madrid would say "good morning" properly, fully pronouncing all the words as, *"muy buenas días."*

But the andaluz simply murmurs *"Mu' buena'"*, eliminating one word wholesale and shortening the others as much as he can get away with.

Similarly, the phrase for swordfish is pronounced carefully in *Castellano* with an emphasis on the "z" in "pez" sounded like a "th" so it sounds like "Pez(th) es-pa-da.

For the andaluz this becomes the much shorter *"pe-pa"*. It's kind of like Cockney shorthand, southern Spanish style.

Hanging with Manolito also pulls me away from the Torremolinos world of the international *extranjeros* and gives me a closer look at the real village people, the year-round residents who don't go away when the warm weather does.

Like Manolito's family, most of them live quite simply in plain homes without a lot of fancy things, or even heating for that matter when winter brings a chill.

One of the winter remedies for cold I discover through them is a metal pan with fiery charcoal in it that you place under a table covered with thick tablecloth. You all sit around the table with you legs tucked under the tablecloth toasting up quite nicely in the heat from the pan.

You have meals this way or just hang around talking and toasting your toes.

Another local custom unfamiliar to me that I learn about is *luto* or mourning.

When somebody in the family of a local dies, the relatives express their sorrow with the way they dress. Women wear all black for whatever the prescribed mourning period is and men wear black armbands. Some time after I meet Manolito, one of his mother's relatives dies and I never again see her in the pretty print dresses she wears at the beginning she wore when I first met her but instead always in black.

The locals I meet with Manolito also dress differently, even when not in mourning. The men tend to dress formally when out about town with suits and ties and the women always wear dresses. Jeans, if they can even get them, are just for the young and well off. Most of my young Spanish friends like Manolito wear real trousers, not jeans.

And shorts, forget that. Nobody wears shorts unless he's a little boy. When a young man hits 12 or 13, the shorts have to go.

Workingmen wear either some version of dark blue mechanic's sort of uniform or the guys who work building sites in summer wear rough white cotton shirts and trousers with these cheap straw and canvas shoes called *alpargatas.*

Duded up and made fashionable these are like the ladies shoes today they call *espadrilles,* but the workingman version is very basic and cheap.

That's pretty much what the local small farmers also wear when we watch them out doing basic chores, like guiding water through their field's irrigated soil furrows by opening and closing dirt channels with crude hoes, much like farmer's have probably done since the early days of the Tigris and Euphrates and Mesopotamia.

Forget tractors and mechanized farms, we are talking donkeys and mules, or teams of oxen for deep plowing.

Old style.

We also get up early in the morning, just after dawn to watch the fishermen from the *Bahondillo* haul in the night's catch.

These are muscular dark-skinned Andaluz's, all the darker for working in the sun. Barefoot, they haul their curved dhow–looking craft up the beach on crude log runners, then put their backs into hauling in the nets.

The catch is silver and wriggling in the new sun and includes a few small sharks and some octopus as well as fish of varying sizes and kinds. Fish monger women with straw baskets haggle and bargain for various bits of the catch to sell later in the town.

These are just some of the scenes Manolito and I come across hanging around together, sort of a tour of what the town has been about for centuries, and not what it is about to become.

Manolito also knows other secrets of the village. What fresh-water *estanque* in the mountains we can go fishing at, who bought a new car, what couple just got engaged, because everybody local knows pretty much about everyone else.

One summer day when we're on the sands of the beach after a round of swimming, my friends point out a young local Spanish kid of about fifteen further down the beach. He wears a white workingman's cap and stands in his bathing suit with his legs awkwardly apart.

"Daybe, you know why he stands like that?" Manolito asks.

I say I'm not sure.

"It's actually because, " one of my other Spanish friends whispers, "He was born up in the Calvario with both a man's and a woman's, *tu sabes*, "things". Everybody knows all about this. But since he can be either sex, he has chosen to live as a man."

Even if you happen to be born a hermaphrodite, there are no secrets in the real Torremolinos, at least not if you know one of the locals like my friend Manolito. Everybody knows all your business, even if it's about the business parts of you.

Summer days when big storms somewhere out in the Mediterranean lash the usual calm waves into real surf, along with Manolito I get to hang with a gang of fisher village kids who teach me how to surf the big waves Torremolinos style.

To this day, I'll happily plunge into any real waves I see, wait out at the surf line for a big one that pulls at you as it comes, and that's a good sign, then swim into it hard as I can.

Catch the wave, pull your arms back against your body, then thrust them down at a thirty degree angle palms flat, and you ride your arms like hydrofoils, body rising part out of the water, head and eyes forward, steering with your arms till the wave deposits you laughing at the sheer joy of it in the foaming shallows.

Another time we wait one sunny afternoon next to the cobble stoned part of the highway leading out of Torremolinos towards Malaga. Manolito has heard the Spanish army will come through on *maniobras*, or maneuvers with *tanques de attaque*, battle tanks.

Sure enough, the ground begins to tremble and shake like an earthquake was happening. And a column of six massive Sherman tanks rounds the village corner and rumbles by spewing black diesel exhaust and shaking the white-washed walls of the local buildings, and causing the few *turistas* who were walking by to wonder if war has broken out.

Hardly something you'd see back in Chevy Chase, Md.

Or there's the time when we see an actual battle, a real gang rumble between the kids of the upper town and the fisherman's kids from the *Bahondillo*. Apparently there is an ancient feud or rivalry between them and some incident or slight has set it off among the younger set. So they are going to settle matters once and for all in a grassy field between the railroad tracks and the highway.

It is later in my years in Torremolinos, so Manolito and I are maybe fourteen or so, too old for this kids fight between 10, 11 and 12 year olds, so we just go as spectators.

There's an electric air of expectant tension in the field as 20 or so upper village kids wait in the middle of the field for their hated fishing village enemies to show their faces if they dare.

The kids carry *palos*, thick sticks for whacking the enemy, plus slings and slingshots, and rocks held in their fists. But the fishing village kids are nowhere in sight. Maybe they're too cowardly to show, *cobardes*.

Suddenly with a mass battle cry, the fishing village kids spring out of their hiding places in bushes and ditches near the railroad tracks.

With slings and slingshots they loose skyward a volley of rocks and, as this rains down on the surprised upper village kids, they charge yelling a battle cry across the field, looking for blood.

After the rocks land, some hitting their marks, the upper village kids respond by hurling their own volley of rocks back at the onrushing gang and then brace to meet the charge. The two sides close with a thwacking of sticks and sharp cries as fists meet faces and thick *palos* whack small angry bodies. It's like some medieval battle, only with children instead of soldiers.

Just when we begin to worry somebody will really get hurt, there is another battle cry from yet another direction. Is it the police?...the Spanish Army?....the kids from other parts of town come to take sides?

No. It's the kids' pissed off mothers, both from the fishing village and the upper town. Screaming with the righteous anger only a mother can summon, they rush in and haul their little sons roughly away by the scruffs of their necks, giving them a better smacking then they were getting from their sworn enemies, and yelling at them to never do this nonsense again, or else.

End of battle.

It's like the movie "West Side Story", the Jets and the Sharks hold a gang rumble, only this time their mommas came out on top.

The fun never ends for Manolito and me.

And so it goes.

Maybe it's ten or so on a sultry summer morning and as the sun's rays heat up the cobblestone street outside, the distant and steady crash of small waves seductively calls every young person to the beach. Or it's the evening of a day just like that, there's a cooling breeze around ten and we've finished a dinner of a local fish called *merluza* and poor man's potatoes with green salad.

Silently, a figure appears on our stone porch and inquires of whomever is visible through the black iron-grated windows:

"Esta *Daybe*?" (Is David in?)

I'm out in a flash, ready for whatever adventure the day or evening has in store for me and Manolito.

Mornings, during summer, we spend at the beach. Before dinner, we might cruise San Miguel during the early evening's *paseo* when everybody's out walking, checking everybody else out.

After dinner, it's the evening *paseo*, doing the same thing with a later crowd, or meeting up with a *pandilla* of kids and shooting the breeze or showing off some fancy bike riding, until its midnight and time to go home.

And the afternoons, the glorious afternoons, are spent in the only real pursuit worthy of our attention: preparing model airplanes at Manolito's house for the glory of flight, under the gentle supervision of his father, Juan, and brother, Juanito.

Besides running the fascist-sanctioned model airplane school for local boys, Manolito's dad also seems to be the unofficial head of the unsanctioned Torremolinos Model Plane Flying Club.

There is no uniform, no dues, no card, no nothing, just a keen interest in building things that fly around you in circles, tethered to control lines and powered by noisy, oily, diesel engines. Radio control at this time and in this country is like a dream, something only a rich man can afford.

But, with very limited means, Manolito's dad, manages to get a miniature air force of his own and others into the sky, piecing aircraft together from bits of this and that. He and Juanito even make their own propellers, carving them carefully out of a hard wood called *"chopo"*, then planing and sanding them down to balanced perfection,

Local enthusiasts come to Juan for advice and repair work. Like this guy Pepe, a local mailman who lives in a small stone sort of farmhouse on the east edge of town and rides one of those cheap red Guzzi motorcycles. Pepe comes by with a large grey thing he's building from scratch, asking for pointers on various construction methods. When I don't recognize the make of the aircraft and ask him what it is, he laughs.

" Oh, it's one of those *cosas* the Americans fly out of Rota air base. You see them all the time. You know. One of those, *tu sabes*, things."

I nod and happily help hold whatever aircraft it is as Juan primes the cylinder head with pungent diesel fuel, then flicks the prop and the engine kicks to life, roaring and bucking and shaking the fuselage of "one of those things" so hard it tickles and jumps in your hand and you're afraid you'll lose your grip on it and it'll fly off across the terrace, destroying everything in its spinning way with the deadly, whirling propeller blades.

Even better are those days when Juan announces the conditions are right for actual flight. The whole afternoon takes on a giddy air of excitement for me as I help with whatever repairs or preparations are necessary, usually involving a fast, navy blue fighter plane called a Grumman Guardian or a light blue Piper Cub kind of thing, with a six foot wingspan, known to us because of it's wide body as "*La Gorda*,"

"The Fat One."

Finally, at around six, when the wind dies down in the evening, we gather up the supplies and the planes and head a quarter of a mile to the same sandy hard dirt field where the circus always sets up when it comes to town.

As if we, too, were some kind of freak circus act, local kids and even grown people see us heading out and follow excitedly to watch the show. On the highway next to the field, buses filled with passengers slow and stop to watch the action. I guess there isn't a lot of real entertainment back then in Torremolinos.

As Juanito, who at 16 already knows how to fly these big things, unwinds the dual control cables and sets up the handgrip, we attach the metal control wires to the wings. Then Juan primes the cylinder head and gets ready to start the engine. The day he motions to me to take over the extremely important job of holding the aircraft correctly while he does this, I am thrilled big time.

A big job like this, and Juan trusts me, a little American kid to do it.

Plus, I have to gently release the howling, vibrating aircraft at the signal of whoever holds the control yoke, then run away quickly before it comes around the circle again and creams me. I feel honored and proud to be chosen for this duty.

But I feel even more so on the day when Juan, standing in the center of the circle as he flies a model around and around him before the admiring crowd, motions to me to join him in the circle. When I do, he shares the control with me and shows me how to gradually turn round and round with the model, keeping your gaze fixed keenly on it.

Around the buzzing aircraft, the clouds in the sky, the trees and the watching crowd become a multi-colored blur, as the aircraft rises and falls with gentle nudges on the control grip. Then Juan lets me hold the grip with him, gradually showing me how to gently control the aircraft with soft, smooth motions.

"*Lento y ligero*. Slow and gentle," he tells me.

Manolito and I both get this lesson quite a few times over many flight days, making brusque, ham-handed mistakes that send the aircraft suddenly diving or lurching drunkenly upwards, saved only by Juan's timely intervention, until we begin to get the vague beginnings of the idea.

Then one afternoon, as we finish up the last of Maruja's *croquetas*, Juan looks over at Juanito and speaks.

"*Esta tarde Manolito y El Daybe vuelan La Gorda.*" Manolito and I are going to fly The Fat One? This afternoon?

A mixture of fear and queasy excitement fill my stomach well beyond all the chicken croquets in the world. What if I crash it? What if I chicken out and run away? What if the engine sputters on takeoff and I stall it? What if, after all my training and love of aircraft, I don't actually have what it takes to fly a plane?

Several nerve-wracking hours later, Manolito has successfully completed his maiden flight with the exception of a bouncy landing that ended up in the bushes at one end of the dusty field.

I'm nervously all alone in the center, clutching the control grip for dear life, my heart practically pounding out of my chest onto the sandy soil as Juan repeatedly flicks the prop on *La Gorda* and she doesn't kick to life.

Maybe she won't start up, maybe I won't have to go through with this after all.

With a deafening roar, the prop turns over and the engine roars to life. Juan adjusts the throttle to a screaming pitch, *La Gorda* bucks and shakes like a fat blue, winged bronco. He looks at me.

I swallow hard, then wiggle the controls up and down, the signal to release her. The Fat One rolls slowly across the field, gaining more and more speed, headed for the bushes, and I tug upwards. Too hard. She lurches shakily into the air in a near stall, as Juan yells to straighten her out which I just manage to do.

I begin to settle down and the world is a blur except for my trembling hand on the control and the soaring blue ship that is *La Gorda,* the large plane pulling so hard I worry it might tug me away with it. Round and round we go until, confident now in my ability, Manolito's dad yells in at me:

"*Daybe. Haz lo que quieras con ella.*

"Do whatever you want with her."

Smiling, I know what to do.

I climb *La Gorda* high, higher, till she's whirling giddily nearly right over my head, the clouds a white blur above her, the whining noise of her engine drowning out the rest of the world.

Then I nose her hard over into a dive, heading straight for the hard, packed ground, she screams higher and louder as she plunges down, faster and faster, nearly going out of control, pulling out over a large craggy rock only at the last possible moment as I nearly miscalculate and wreck The Fat One.

Juan's voice laughs out:

"Pero, ten cuidado. 'But be careful'. "

A few more circles and *La Gorda's* engine splutters out of fuel. I hold my breath as she glides silently earthwards and as I guide her gently, gently down to a landing as smooth and perfect as any I have ever imagined, there's a cheer from the crowd standing around and even from the people on the buses that stopped to watch the little homegrown air show.

"Bien hecho, Daybe", Juan shouts approvingly.

And, while Juan and Juanito congratulate me on my baptism of flight, my good friend Manolito runs over yelling happily and shakes my arm, I know exactly what he's thinking.

We feel like we've been anointed with diesel fuel and confirmed as real air men. Sort of a coming of age Bar Mitzvah of the sky.

My Davey Crockett life and boyish All-American dreams back in Bethesda may have faded smaller in the far distance. But this day, here in Torremolinos, I stand tall and proud. I am not quite sure who I am or what country I am from, but I do feel today I am definitely someone.

David M. Johnson

11
La Mimi

"RIA RIA-PI<u>TA</u>! RIA RIA-PI<u>TA</u>!"

Over and over again the amply plump flamenco teacher repeats this simple rhythmic phrase.

As she does, she clicks together a pair of wooden castanets in each hand in time to the words, starting with the pinky finger and working her way up her fingers and back down again with each syllable, *"ri-a ri-a-pi-ta!"*, standing proudly with her back arched.

Behind her, a window on the bare wood-floored second floor room looks out on the Plaza Central up above a dusty bar that has been there forever.

In front of her, twenty budding Carmens, ranging in age from eight to 14 or so, arch their backs in imitation and hold their heads as high and haughty as little girls can hope to manage.

They lift their castanet-clad hands, and slowly repeat the exercise, drowning the room in a ragged cascade of castanet clicks as they repeat the magic phrase.

"Ria ria-pita! Ria ria-pita!"

The instructress takes in the cacaphonous din and the little girls make contorted faces as they struggle to coax clicks from their castanets. She smiles. As the noise of tiny voices and wood hitting wood reaches a crescendo, she claps her hands twice for attention.

"Muy bién. Y ahora "La Sevillana".

She goes over to an ancient record player, turns it on and drops the needle on a slightly warped 45 record. The tinny sounds of a *"La Sevillana"* struggle out, rising in pitch every time the warped part of the disc spins around to lift the needle.

On the floor of the room, twenty little señoritas stamp and whirl through the prescribed paces of a 300-year-old dance, mostly with dark eyes flashing from faces framed in jet black Spanish hair. Except there are a few *"rubias"* here and there, whose blonde or *"rubia"* hair sets them apart from the rest of the troupe.

One of these is my little sister, "La Mimi."

Back in Chevy Chase she would have been in ballet class or learning to waltz or maybe even taking square dance lessons and trying out a little "doseydo" action. This is not an era when young ladies are encouraged to even think about anything in the way of sports for developing their bodies.

In the U.S., soccer doesn't even exist for girls or boys and, as for baseball, you'd have to be kidding, that's strictly *macho* territory.

No, this is a time when young ladies who want to get out and move their stuff around are led straight to dance class.

And, here in España, that means clicking castanets, cries of *"ria riapita"* and unfamiliar dances with names like *"La Malagueña," La Sevillana"* and *"las burlerías."*

Nothing your average young American girl is ever likely to encounter.

But, since she has, "La Mimi" gets right into it.

She stamps her little feet and looks angry with the best of them.

In a flash, she raises her arms, clicks the castanets on cue, then whirls back into the dance. For a nine-year-old, you might say she has what the Spaniards call *duende.*

Although literally translated the word means "fairy" as in, you know, Tinkerbelle, in this flamenco sense it's the closest Spanish equivalent to the American word "soul", as in "that chick's got *soul*, man."

Duende.

And "La Mimi", despite being born and bred in US suburbia, seems to have her share of Spanish *duende.*

When *Holiday* magazine (eventually *Holiday/Travel*) does a piece on the Costa del Sol, the entire flamenco class stages a dance for them on the stone porch and steps of the Torremolinos church. As the tiny señoritas whirl and stamp beneath the church's cross and belfry's, the magazine's photographer clicks away like mad.

A few months later, it's "La Mimi's" picture that graces the photo spread in the magazine with the following caption:

"This tiny Carmen is ready for a fling at the flamenco. Despite all the airs and graces of Spain, she is Mimi Johnson, 8, of Washington, D.C."

Perhaps inspired by that photographic honor, Mimi does something daring when it's time to pick out fabric for this year's flamenco dress.

The students are sent to the dark shop of the *modista*, or tailor, in downtown Málaga, a cluttered place full of bolts of cloth and tailor's dummies with needles sticking everywhere like vaguely human pin cushions.

The usual flamenco dress choices are set variations on the same basic theme: polka dots on a solid field. These are usually either white on red, red on white, or some combination of green or blue or maybe yellow, and so on, but almost always polka dots.

But, flagrantly ignoring tradition, "La Mimi" opts for something bolder, yet more severe, as befitting a truly serious *bailaora*.

Solid gold with jet-black trim. No polka dots.

If the *modista* had sewn her a complete outfit as the Queen of England, complete with tiara and authentic crown jewels, she could not be more proud of that dress. Years later, as a grownup, Mimi tells me that dress is one of those select few pieces of wardrobe that, in a lifetime of buying clothes, a woman remembers as absolutely perfect and pure and instantly cherished.

That gold and black trimmed dress lives in her heart forever, long after the garment itself has vanished into memory like a cool Mediterranean sea mist blown away by the hot *sirocco* winds from Africa.

Flamenco indeed seems to touch something Spanish in my little sister's soul.

A little bit of *duende* deep in her *alma*.

She is even invited to attend her teacher's wedding, a full blown church event she will always remember for one very unusual fact: the groom isn't actually there.

Like many young men in this job-poor country, he's away working illegally in Germany where he can earn some real money, but can't come back to Spain and return to Germany again without a work visa.

So the couple gets married by proxy. Standing in for the groom during the ceremony is his best friend Miguel, the *practicante*, or local doctor in training. Presumably, up in Germany some *fraulein* is doing the same for the bride. Weird, but that's life in Spain at this time.

Unpredictably, when it comes to other aspects of life in Torremolinos, my sister fights to stay as American as possible. This is the beginning of a long battle with my mother who is determined her daughter be raised as a proper, elegantly mannered Spanish *señorita*, "not some common, gum-chewing American girl," which when you consider who we are, she pretty much should be.

I mean, who exactly are we as a family, the Astors? Hardly. Neither of my parents went to college, they worked their way up from airline clerks into the middle class but that's it.

My step grandfather, the David Johnson I'm named for, was a semi-literate Swedish farm boy immigrant who made his living buying up old houses in San Francisco, fixing them up and selling them.

My Welsh born great grandfather Thomas Williams listed his profession as "slate miner" when he enlisted at 16 in the Union Army in Philadelphia during the Civil War, thereby earning his American citizenship.

Hardly silk stocking stuff.

Why his great granddaughter Mimi should be groomed as a lofty *señorita* kind of defies any logic but my mother's. Maybe my mother's is making my sister do penance for her own deep shame that her dad lost all his money in the Depression, or for the humiliation of being an airline clerk instead of going to college, who really knows.

This continues later, when we live in Madrid, and Mark and I are sent to an American high school. Instead Mimi must attend instead a Spanish school where she supposedly will become a señorita, despite her howls of protest and tears. My mother stands firm.

Even back in Torremolinos she warns Mimi to avoid a fate worse than *la muerte* itself:

"You don't ever want to be like one of those cheap little American girls that stand there like little dopes and make noises with their chewing gum like 'smack! smack smack!' all day."

Gosh, yeah. A terrible fate.

In response, my sister chews gum every chance she gets, refuses to hang out with the local Spanish kids, not even the ones in her dance class, and instead spends all the time she can with American girlfriends, preferably enjoying their drink of choice.

Coca Cola.

Take that. *Señora*!

For "La Mimi" a perfect Torremolinos afternoon is spent at home with a friend like Ceci Riddell or Missy Ericson, both all American girls from California no less. They sit on the floor and play a board game called "Careers". In this day and age it seems to heavily direct young ladies towards becoming secretaries, homemakers or teachers. The doctor, lawyer thing just isn't happening yet for girls.

As they play, by their side they like to have a package of the hard butter cookies called Galletas María.

And ice-cold Coca Colas.

Their conversation often turns to things they miss the most about America. Like real hamburgers. Television. Soft toilet paper (the Spanish version *Elefante* being about the consistency of brown package wrapping paper). And that most wonderful American marvel of all time: cake mixes.

"Guy, it's stupid!" Ceci will moan. "How can you make a simple chocolate cake when you have to buy all these ingredients and mix them together forever. What's the matter with these Spaniards, don't they know anything?!"

Or in hot weather, they go to the beach and sun themselves. At lunchtime, that means going to the thatch covered patio at Antonio's restaurant and getting a plate of *huevos fritos*, two freshly laid fried eggs with heaps of hot french fries cooked in olive oil, or even better some *chanquetes*, the local delicacy of breaded, fried minnows, eaten whole by the handful.

Heaven, with a side of Coca Cola.

In the evening, they take the *paseo* and stroll up the Calle San Miguel to the stand that sells *patatas fritas*, freshly-fried potato chips wrapped in newspaper. Or they go together to the Cinema Universal, and see movies. American movies, of course. Things with warbling, dubbed-in-Spanish soundtracks, but from the good old USA nonetheless.

Here's the part about *La Mimi* that really burns me up as we get a little older. You have to be fourteen years old to see a lot of the movies they show, and that means most of the really neat ones, with whatever sexy bit that slips by the village priest or gunfire action or bloodthirsty vampires.

If you don't look fourteen, the guy at the door doesn't let you in. No i.d.'s or stuff. It's all up to him.

And by the time she's eleven or so, Mimi has grown taller than me and apparently looks old enough with a little lipstick to just waltz right in. She glances back at me with a smile.

The man at the door looks me over, shakes his head and says I'm no way old enough. I can't follow Mimi in.

I want to grab this guy and shake him.

"I'm nearly thirteen, you *idiota!* You just let my little sister in, if you think she's old enough you blind, old bat, you've got to give me a break, *hombre!*"

These are the kind of injustices in life that just about destroy a man. It is hard enough having a little sister to start with.

In the beginning, there is just Mark and me. He's older and therefore bigger, so he has all the Big Boy "Mommy, Daddy, look how fast I can run and jump!" stuff covered.

So what. As the younger kid, I can always out-cute him. Where he is always bigger, I can be more charming, little boy appealing. "Isn't that so cute, dear, look what the little guy is doing now."

It works. We each have our place, our reasons for being. Life is good.

Then along comes someone who wasn't just cuter than me by virtue of being younger, she's a girl to boot. That's like cuteness squared, to the N-th power.

I am dead. I have nowhere to go on this one. No way can I compete.

Now some low-paid, moron of a Spanish cinema employee in a town at the ends of the Earth has to tell me that my sister isn't just younger and cuter than me. She's also <u>older</u> and cuter than me.

Arrrrrggggghhhhhh!!!!!!!!

Maybe you can therefore understand why, one day when she's a bit older, I'm inspired to come up with an idea, a special plan. And how I convince my brother we have a secret mission to accomplish.

Kill Mimi's dolls.

This is the way it works. We share a second-floor bedroom next to Mimi's in a house in front of the church. Both bedrooms have wrought-iron balconies close enough to each other so you can just manage to climb from one to another without falling and breaking a leg, which given the twenty foot drop you would or worse. This is to be our escape route. We just have to bide our time for Mimi to go out for a while.

The minute she does, we scurry into her bedroom with a big ball of twine and some scissors. With some careful arrangement, we tie strings to all of her dolls and put them in mortal peril. Just tug on the string and one doll will fall into a bucket of water and drown, another will topple over a cliff (her dresser, actually), another will be hanged. And so on.

Here's the really diabolical part. We are not going to pull the strings and kill her dolls. Not us. No way. That would be wrong.

She will.

You see, her door opens outwards. All we have to do is tie all the strings to the knob of the closed door, sneak our way out her balcony to ours, and wait, laughing maniacally, for her return.

Soon, we see her come innocently back up the street. There is a sound of soft footsteps coming up the stairs. And of her latch being turned. There is a moment of silence.

A high, bloodcurdling scream pierces the afternoon.

And all of La Mimi's dolls are dead. And she herself has done the deed, with her own hand. Us? We were innocently in our room. Doing nothing. Nothing.

My mother somehow doesn't see it quite that way. Failing to see the humor and ingenuity in the Great Dead Doll caper, she sees to it Mark and I are forced to spend more time than we actually had planned to in our room with the balcony.

Somehow, for me, Little Mister Too Young for the Movies, it's worth it.

Besides, my sister's growing older. It's probably time La Mimi put her dolls away anyway. And concentrated on older things. Maybe we were doing her a favor.

By the time she is twelve or thirteen, she does get beyond dolls. Boys notice her and vice versa. One evening, when we are living in a house with a private garden overlooking the sea, she lets Pacquito Flores give her a kiss. Somehow the news gets back to the *Señora* and she is not pleased. Mark and I may have something to do with it.

Perhaps we are protecting her from a local Romeo notorious for going after *extranjeras* for a little action the Spanish girls won't give. Perhaps we don't like him because he is a wise ass. *Quien sabe?* Who can say?

A year more and Mimi begins to fall in at last with a group of Spanish kids, but not from the village. She meets them at the beach past the *La Carihuela,* near a restaurant/pool club called the El Remo. They are summer kids, the children of well-to-do people from Madrid. She likes the girls and, apparently, the boys see some kind of *duende* or other in this little *americana.*

So she falls in with their little gang, what they call in Spain a *pandilla.*

And she attends their *guateques,* parties where they dance to American music by people like Chuck Berry and Elvis Presley and they drink Coca Cola.

This is about as far as she dives into the Spanish thing.

Years later, Mimi can't even remember actual Spanish boyfriends I tell her about. Or many events in Torremolinos

So she never really fulfilled my mother's vision that she would become a perfect little aristocratic Spanish señorita, arching her back with haughty grace and clicking her wooden castanets at the adoring crowd with a rhythmic:

"Ria ria-pita!"

12
El Cura

AN EVENING BREEZE RUSTLES the many fragrant nispero trees and eucalyptus bushes and all the flowering cacti.

Paul Anka is singing *"Oh, please stay by me, Diana."* over some fuzzy speakers hanging from the white-washed walls that enclose a makeshift outdoor theater next to where the train tracks cross *la carretera* at the south side of town.

To Paul's accompaniment there is the steady crack, crack cracking, then spit, spit, spitting of several hundred people expertly putting a *pipa*, or salted sunflower seed, in their mouth, deftly placing it between their teeth with their tongues for the swift bite that cracks the shell apart.

A little more tongue work and that tasty, fat sunflower seed is separated from the salty shells which get spat outward and down so as not hit the movie patron in the folding chair in front, while you enjoy the oily seed and the salty residue left by the shells.

Gradually, the loose pebble floor of this garden-cinema becomes covered with expelled *pipa* seeds.

There is no butter for the movie house popcorn, heck there is no popcorn, no Good and Plenty, no Jujy fruits, no Raisinettes. And no movie house. Just a flower garden with a makeshift screen and for snacks: sunflower seed *pipas* and strangely colorful Spanish hard candies, hand-wrapped in see-through cellophane, and sold by roving vendors.

The Spanish version of the classic movie refreshment stand is as foreign to me as the notion of an outdoor theater.... without cars and detachable speakers.

The bare light bulbs strung around the walls and in the trees go off, and the screen flickers to life, as a warbling soundtrack struggles from 0 to 60, not very quickly, and a narrator begins talking in rapid Spanish.

We are first treated to something called a "No Do". That doesn't mean an actionless film or one of those warnings to the audience against inappropriate behavior, like "no do" talking and "no do" to forget to turn cell phones off (yeah, right, this is 1957, guys).

"No Do" means *Noticías Documentarías*, or documentary news. But it's not real documentary like Public TV or Michael Moore today. It's more like government propaganda, in fact, it basically is.

Most of it seems to be about Franco or other people in uniforms or church robes, either military or the regalia of high church officials. I don't yet know enough Spanish to fully get it, but apparently Franco is opening a dam somewhere and people are happy about it because they are clapping deliriously.

Then Franco is shaking someone's hand at some sort of agricultural show where there are huge pigs and cows. Then some generals are reviewing troops and congratulating each other about something or other, after which Spanish planes drop bombs on a cornfield as soldiers and tanks maneuver about.

This all accompanied by stirring action kind of music with trumpets and drums and the like.

It doesn't seem very interesting to me, nor for that matter to the audience which keeps talking quietly, ignoring the screen and Franco's many accomplishments, to keep crack, crack, cracking *pipas*.

After far too much of this we thankfully get to the main feature, something billed in the posters outside as *"El Mundo Del Circo,"* but which we know from the smaller type to be "Big Top" with Burt Lancaster.

I'm looking forward to seeing a familiar American face, hearing some real English spoken, in this land of strange things like *pipas* and pebble-floored outdoor theaters that lack cars and Jujy fruits, where the only familiar Stateside thing is Paul Anka singing sadly about this older woman called "Diana."

And Paul doesn't fully count anyway as genuine USA because he's Canadian. Close, but no cigar.

At last the movie starts.

Soon suddenly onscreen here's our guy Burt, not dressed as a American cowboy like I remember seeing him in "The Gunfighter," but in those circus acrobat tights, still a real muscular USA hero nonetheless, an authentic piece of where I came from. Burt strides into the scene and opens his mouth to let somebody know something or other, his lips move.

And I don't believe it.

Burt has learned to speak Spanish!

Only, it doesn't sound at all like him at all. It's a deeper, faster voice. In fact, if you watch it for a while, his lips don't even move right. I can't begin to understand it.

Then Tony Curtis comes in and he's doing the Spanish thing, too. Gone is the Brooklyn accent, now he's like from Madrid or Sevilla or somewhere. My God, this couldn't get weirder.

But it does.

Somewhere, after everybody rattles on in Spanish and runs about doing things, and the story develops, it gets time for that mushy bit I always cringe at, the dopey guy/girl part, the kiss scene.

You know it's coming. You can kind of tell when the man and the woman are yelling like they can't stand the sight of each other, but they keep stealing glances anyway. Then the man comes over to her and they glare at each other real hard. Then he takes her hand and pulls her roughly to him and they press together and....

Wham!

It's the next morning. They never kissed.

Sure, they're smiling and cooing and beaming at each other like something went on. Only nothing did, at least on screen, because I was looking and cringing, waiting for the icky mush, and it never came.

And, in Torremolinos, while I was there, it never will. There is no kissing in Torremolinos, not on screen, never happens, for one supremely powerful reason.

El cura.

The village priest.

This is the church's town when it comes to stuff like that and the strict catholic rule on the movie-kissing thing is as unyielding as those ragged nails holding an agonized Christ to the Cross in the bloody statue in church.

No way does anybody, no matter how big a Hollywood star, get to kiss somebody else in the movie unless they're properly married and flaunting wedding rings to prove it.

I know, because when the new indoor Cine Universal opens to great fanfare near the other railroad crossing at Calle San Miguel, and there are now movies year round, I see tons of movies, but no kisses.

I can still remember some great set-ups for them. Clark Gable and Ava Gardner in "Mogambo,", hating each other deep in the untamed wilds of Africa yet wanting each other so bad like a pair of love crazed African lions that one night they are simply drawn together in the jungle heat and....

Wham! It's tomorrow morning.

John Wayne and Angie Dickinson in "Rio Bravo." It's evening and the big sky is lit up like a crimson fire, John moves in for a kiss behind the old covered wagon and....

Pow! Everybody's mounting up as the wagon train hits the trail the following day.

Tony Curtis going for Janet Leigh in "The Viking", in a torch lit stone walled castle chamber and....

Zap! Sorry, Tony. We had to douse your flaming hot torch and cut to some fake-looking model Viking ships plowing through a "North Sea" storm in some water filled studio tank.

Talk about throwing cold water on it.

I guess the bright side of being protected from all those nasty, non-catholic kisses is that I no longer have to cringe at the mooshy parts in the movies. But they make some weird cuts and continuity leaps. Sometimes when you think you know where the story is headed then abruptly leap forward a scene or two, your mind reels and spins, like a reel on a movie projector that's spun past the end and flaps noisily, your puzzled brain desperately trying to fill in the blanks.

"What?....but I thought... how come they didn't, uh?....."

Not actually being either a Catholic or a true part of the village, born and bred there, I mostly never really see the full effect the priest has on things other than movie stories, like how he affects daily life, what you can and cannot do.

For us foreign kids he is a man wearing a weird robe or even a woman's dress that you see leading the Holy Week processions through the village, surrounded by men in sort of Klu Klux Klan get ups.

Or, if you sneak into church during mass, you hear him solemnly intoning some scary unknown things in Latin while altar boys swing metal incense burners from chains, clouding the church with a sickly sweet smelling fog, creating the kind of spooky mist Dracula emerges from in those movies that don't have kisses.

Or we follow funeral processions from the church to the cemetery high above the sea at the top of the cliffs, the bereaved family and friends looking hollow-eyed and shell-shocked, and the priest's the one moaning the burial stuff while we sneak around and look at the pile of bones of people whose families no longer can pay the church rent on their burial plots.

One time though I get to see him do the censorship thing he did in movies in a big, real life situation.

There is a young French lady who works at the Berlitz school next door to us when we are living in front of the church. She is dark haired, friendly, very pretty, and fond of sunning herself, something my brother and I discover she does, in private on the roof adjoining ours, shielded by towels strung from a line.

Usually she is in this skimpy French swimsuit called a bikini, the kind of thing nobody wears on a Spanish beach back in 1957.

And, on certain heavenly occasions, she sheds the bikini top which, of course, particularly explains why Mark and I contrive reasons to sneak up the stairs in dead silence and peer at her through cracks in the towels, holding our breath least she hear us as we contemplate paradise, or at least the French subtitled version.

I don't know if she knows we are there or even cares. I'm sure things are looser in France, where by then the bikini is no big deal.

But not in 1950s Spain. That is what causes the shit to hit the Holy fan.

One day she actually wears the bikini...to the beach.

Ay Díos!

Picture about thirty fishermen in their black berets, pants rolled up, barefoot and sitting on their haunches in the sand in a wide circle. At the center of that entranced circle, maybe ten feet from any of them, and where their eyes are all riveted, is the young French lady, eyes closed and skin oiled up, sunning herself on a towel.

In her bikini!

The fishermen don't speak. They don't move. They just watch grinning politely.

We are talking about a Spain where there is no Playboy magazine. Where Post Office censors rip offending pages out of foreign magazines before they are delivered. Where there is no kissing in the movies, even if you are Clark Gable in the heat of darkest Africa.

And there are absolutely no bikinis on the sands of Spanish beaches.

None. *Ninguno.*

This is as close as these poor fishermen are likely to get to seeing a young woman's naked body, other than their wives, of course, and then who knows whether they let the lights be on or not.

The French girl might as well be buck-naked.

At least that's how the priest sees it.

There is a commotion and shouting from above the beach, coming closer along the rough dirt road that leads from the village above down to the hot sands.

This commotion sounds like the shrieking furies themselves.

Down marches the fuming priest, head held high, accompanied on either side by a green suited Guardia Civil, machine guns strapped to their shoulders, black patent leather boots marching with purpose.

He strides up to the startled young woman, he's yelling and purple in the face.

Grabbing up a towel he hurls it roughly over her body and, head held high to regard the heavens rather than to view her sinful oiled up flesh, he angrily points her off the beach, looking for all the world like one of those silent movie villains ordering the heroine out of the cabin into the blinding snowstorm.

And the *guardias* lead her off, preserving once again the purity of the sand from the apparent impurity of the bikini-clad French female flesh.

Hey, this is history. I get to see the first bikini on the *Costa Del Sol* and the first holy cow reaction to it.

I really only remember one other thing about the village *cura*. This is when we are living in the same house in front of the church where we spy on the unfortunate bikini girl French "strumpet."

In the afternoons and early evening, lots of kids hang out in the street by the side of the church doing things kids do in the street. There is a door by the side that leads to the priest's home and sometimes he comes out and talks to the kids, like any other neighbor, only the other neighbor guys wear pants, not dresses.

Over time, the priest gets to talking to, among other kids, my brother Mark who stands out from the other kids with his angelic blond hair. The priest asks him about America and things and whatever. And one day he feels neighborly enough to Mark to suggest my brother ask our mother if the priest can have him up to tea.

I believe my mother is very pleased and honored that the village priest would extend such an invitation to Mark and agrees, sending him over in nice clean clothes, hair combed and the rest.

Nothing big really happens at the tea. Mark gets to see where the priest lives, meets his mother who lives with him and they are to have some tea and *galletas* and talk.

But one thing Mark says on returning to our house, struck him as odd, and it stays with me all these years.

While Mark is there the priest's mother goes off somewhere to get the tea and cookies and the priest continues showing off his quarters.

He tells Mark he has some very special books and takes him over to a dark little alcove to see them, laying a friendly arm on my brother's shoulder as he talks about them.

Mark thinks nothing of it.

Then, without warning, the priest's mother silently returns. And she barks her son's name, sharply, like a whiplash.

"Antonio!"

At the sound of her voice, the priest rips his arm off Mark's shoulder like it was on fire and jumps back with a guilty cry of surprise and a frightened look at his mother, the *padre's* left panting and gasping for air.

Mark says the priest's mother shoots her son a fierce and angry look, a look that could kill a man dead. Mark feels "something is really wrong here".

And that's it. Not such a big deal.

But here's my take on it.

Maybe that *cura* has the holy power back then to cut what he believes is sin out of the movies. And rail against it in Latin during mass. And enlist cops to cover Satan's French mademoiselle vile lust with towels, and drive sin disguised as a young woman off the beach, sending it back to Frenchie hell where the church doctrine affirms it belongs.

But there must have be some part of it, some mocking hidden vein of sin sparked by the sight of young blond boys, that for all his Latin and praying and piety, the *cura* couldn't snip out of himself.

And drop like a forbidden kiss on the cutting room floor.

Torremolinos

13
El Miko

A SMALL CAMPFIRE FLICKERS way out in the vast desert wastelands. Around it sit two desperate looking men. One of them, a mean-looking, scar-faced *americano,* laughs about the bank job they just pulled. The notion that he just shot dead a bank cashier means nothing to him.

Nor does the fact that, while running out of the bank, he collides with a young boy who accidentally pulls his mask off. The act of bashing the boy's head in with a rock is routine.

The stupid brat looked at his face. The boy had to die.

That's all.

A young Mexican woman they have taken captive comes to stoke the fire. As she leans over the fire, her skirt silhouettes the curves of her comely young body. The scar-faced one eyes her hungrily.

He takes a long pull at the whiskey bottle, and grabs her wrist. When she resists, he stands up and, seizing her roughly, hauls her into a nearby mining shack, oblivious to her frightened cries.

At the fire his partner in crime, Pedro, the Mexican bandit, laughs like a simpleton at the silly antics of his gringo companion.

He does not laugh for long.

Creeping from behind a bush, the father of the dead boy closes in on the laughing Mexican, pistol held tight by the barrel.

Whack!

He clubs the bandit with the butt of the gun, and Pedro, the treacherous Mexican desperado, collapses like a punctured balloon, sliding down dead into a ravine.

Seething with revenge for his murdered little boy, the father looks towards the door of the mining shack. His eyes narrow in determination, then he turns at the sound of a voice.

"Okay, cut! Good, Mike. Now we set up the scene where 'The Scar' comes out, he sees you, you both draw and you shoot him dead. Then you'll take the young Mexican woman by the hand and lead her off into the sunset."

El Miko has spoken.

That's *El Miko* as in my big brother, Mark. This day he's also *El Miko*, the Great Hollywood director, and we are his players. He's standing there winding up his Kodak 8-milimeter camera for the next scene of his epic western "The Scar."

"Mike," or Michael Dorner, smiles and nods. The fact that the young Mexican woman happens to be his sister, Lisa, is unimportant. This is filmmaking and their family is actually in the business. In fact, their older cousin, Paula Weinstein, will one day head a major Hollywood studio.

But today we are making, not a big Hollywood film, but a "spaghetti Western" years before Clint Eastwood ever rode onto to the Spanish film scene in "A Fistful of Dollars" which will be shot just outside Madrid in the 1960s.

I dust myself off and climb back up the ravine. Thanks to my sombrero and the beach towel draped over my shoulder, I'm obviously Pedro, the Mexican. Or was. Only now I'm dead. Just like Dana, who played the bank cashier, and little Danny Dorner, the kid whose head got bashed in.

A few scenes later my sister Mimi, the evil dance hall girl, gets hers when she tries to stab Mike from behind and Lisa shoots her dead. An *El Miko* production seems to require more than a few dead bodies.

Many weeks later, after the Kodak lab in Gibraltar sends back the processed film, *El Miko* has a premiere of "The Scar" in our private "screening room" (actually a barren third floor room just below our fourth floor "scientific laboratory").

The only soundtrack is the clatter of the Kodak projector, the occasional hoots of laughter from the gathered kids, and the tinny warbling music from a 45rpm disc on a cheap turntable.

This is way before mini-cams or easily affordable home movies with soundtracks. We're lucky it's in color at all: many early *El Miko* efforts are in black and white.

In our dark screening room, in this slightly garish Kodacolor, the eyebrow pencil "scar" on bad guy Mike Stevens doesn't seem quite as amateurish as it did in real life. Maybe the acting does, but we don't care.

It's a movie. And we made it.

This has been going since the Christmas 1957 when Mark unwraps his present, sent from Dad all the way back in America, and finds the movie camera. Three days later on his birthday, he unwraps a projector from the same source. And he is off to the movies, thanks to good old Dad.

It's hard to believe that the same loving father-in-absentia, who sent him these wonderful play things, will years later try to discourage him from pursuing movies as a career. Threatening to cut off payment on college tuition if Mark studies any cinema at all instead of business which is what "real men study," our father lays it out for him, probably after more than a few martinis.

"I'll be damned if I'll pay for any son of mine to study anything as silly as the movies. It's no place for a decent young man. You should study business, real business. I lived in Los Angeles and I know what the movies are all about. To make it in Hollywood you have to be a Jew. Or a fag."

Well, Dad, at least you bought him the camera and the projector. It was a start and it came from the right place.

Because somehow in Torremolinos *El Miko* falls in love with the movies. Maybe it happpens while he watches some badly dubbed American feature in the town's outdoor, orchard garden movie house that first summer.

Or maybe he is caught up in the town's feverish excitement when Torremolino's first real indoor cinema begins to be built next to the train tracks heading towards Málaga.

For months, everyone follows its construction, as a large pink and white stucco building begins to take shape. Adorning the front of it, a three-dimensional hemisphere of the earth from space, crudely done in plaster and painted blue and green. Surrounding this depiction of the whole entire world, the grand title of this fine building:

"Cine Universal."

Wow. The cinema.... of the entire universe! Here in the little village of Torremolinos.

And when it opens, the entire world is there, including of course *El Miko*. In order to make the opening date, the building still is only half painted and lacks stucco here and there. But that first night rivals all the glamour and excitement of any Hollywood premiere, everyone in town stands in line for hours to attend a showing.

Perhaps this is where and why Mark falls in love with movies. Or maybe it's because, like airplanes did for me, it fills a void in him, supplying something he desperately misses from back home.

Like, for instance, America itself.

Almost all of the movies we see are American. The voices may be crudely dubbed by Spanish actors and the dialogue re-written and censored by the authorities (A few years later in "West Side Story", the insult: "Why don't you go walk the streets like your sister," becomes, thanks to the Franco era censors, the less salacious "why don't you go fry some asparagus.")

But going to the movies is like taking that boat back across the Atlantic for a couple of hours and actually being in the States.

Many decades later Mark will recall there was something even deeper in his psyche about his trips to the movies over there, so far from America: he remembers feeling that, there in the cool darkness of a Spanish cinema, our father was almost there sitting in the seat next to him, holding the popcorn, and not 5,000 miles away.

The movies were for Mark a cure for the cold and lonely void left by our father's absence.

Even if that's part of it and movies are some sort of missing connection for him, it goes deeper for *El Miko* than love of flying does for me.

When we grow up, I will put airplanes away as part of childhood and they will not play a role in my adult world. El Miko will make movies his life.

He also discovers girls in Torremolinos. Some of the local village girls catch his eye and, like me, *El Miko* finds his attention drawn to them.

There's one dark-haired young lady who works at the shoe cobbler's on the *Calle San Miguel*. She has a flashing smile, tanned skin and long hair. Somehow *El Miko* finds himself often in need of shoe repairs or a shoeshine or new laces. He even makes friends with the young boy who works there just so he can stop by to visit and maybe say a word or two to the young lady.

Another of his local friends lives in a farmhouse right by the sea in front of the Bahondillo fishing village. One night he invites Mark to a christening party for one of his baby sisters.

At the party all the kids drink wine and, being Spanish and accustomed to it, they handle it well. Not Mark. At twelve years old he staggers home so stinking drunk, he can barely walk, and my mother and sister put him fully clothed into a cold shower.

There's also the social scene at the Cine Universal. Before the lights go out and the newsreel begins to impart news of Generalisimo Franco's latest accomplishments, the boys size up the girls and vice versa. Maybe if you are brave enough after the show, you might say a few words to the one you fancy before you head your separate ways home. That's about it at this stage of the game.

"El Miko" playing it cool with older, unattainable, Laurie Riddell
who he never told back then he had a huge crush on.

El Miko also discovers the erotic side of the fair sex: hard to do in a catholic Spain where there are no Playboys on the news stands.

Somehow, on our various visits to English-ruled Gibraltar, Mark discovers that this rather raunchy port town offers a supply of pornography for the sailors passing through.

He begins to make excuses while we are there, going off to look for something or other. One time he returns with a deck of cards featuring nude women in various "artistic" poses. Another time he brings back a black and white English magazine featuring all nude shots of sailor's dream girls with their private parts airbrushed over, so that they are as well-equipped for action as say a bunch of my sister's anatomically incorrect plastic Barbie dolls.

Still, for a small group of boys in Torremolinos, they provide plenty to gawk at and mull over, page after titillating page.

One day, our American friend Dana comes in with news that sweeps *El Miko's* English porno mag under the bed and away from our attention.

Tomorrow morning, the circus is coming!

Halleluhah. White hot sparks. *Chispas!*

This is a once-a-year event that sets the pulse racing of every single kid in town. A real live circus! Even for movie-struck Mark, Hollywood itself for a while seems to pale by comparison.

El Miko doesn't care that it's a kind of tattered traveling affair, with holes in the tent and stitched up places in the tights of the trapeze lady.

It's a circus, man! And, it's not just any circus, it's the *Circo Ruso*, the Russian Circus with performers and acts straight from Mother Russia!

This is international show biz on its highest level.

And, if a kid like Mark notices that last year these same performers come through, not as the Russian Circus, but as the *Circo Americano*, the American Circus, he doesn't care.

So what if the guy who, last year, was the buckskin-wearing Old West marksman "Boofalo Beel," who shot a lit cigarette from the mouth of an Indian maiden, this year he's miraculously now the Cossack-clad marksman Ivan Ivanovich who shoots a cigarette from the mouth of a pink tight-clad Russian Cossackette who looks suspiciously like last year's frankly plump Indian girl.

C'mon. It's the circus! It's show biz!

Mark knows from last year's show that this tattered rag tag two bit travelling circus with its patched up tent and cobbled together show still somehow summons real magic powers.

He can be sure that when he sits again on the crude wood plank bench seats and the lights dim and the rest of the world fades, this brightly lit circus ring will take him somewhere far away from our little lives in exile.

When that little circus band launches into a bouncy mambo tune like Perez Prado's "Patricia", and the pretty lady in the pink tights climbs the thick white velvet-wrapped rope that the very impossibly muscular guy is holding... something magical begins to happen.

As she wraps one leg around the rope and holds her arms and other leg out fearlessly to the crowd, and the buff guy twirls the rope faster and faster and the trumpets and clarinet wail about "Patricia' and the white hot spotlight shows the spinning woman is a whirling blur of a legs-arms legs-arms legs-arms kaleidoscope it seems like the portal to an enchanted world has been momentarily pried open.

Suddenly the wildly spinning lady loosens her leg on the rope and slides dangerously down at breakneck speed and you and the audience gasp and hold its collective breath, fearing the beautiful young woman will be dashed to the ground and badly injured.

When at the last minute she somehow breaks her fall, the spell too is broken and you cheer wildly. In your soul you know you've just been transported for a few heartbeats to a land far, far away.

That's what the circus is bringing. And if you want to help, kid, you can apparently be a part of it.

Mark is in.

Early the next morning Mark. and every kid in town show up at the same dusty field where Manolito's dad takes me to fly planes. Rumors rise and fall that the circus trucks have been sighted.

Suddenly, there's a shout from down the highway. The kid who works at the cobbler's has been waiting there as a scout. Now he waves his beret excitedly and cries out.

"Allí vienen! Allí vienen." There they come!

Up the coastal highway they advance, gearboxes grinding. Gaily painted circus trucks and buses, lumbering one after another onto the dust and bushes of the field. The circus is here and Mark is going to help them set up. Supposedly they will pay kids to help.

There is plenty to do. Piles of stakes and rope have to be unloaded from trucks. The canvas of the tent has to be hauled out, carried into position and then rolled open.

Various trailers have to be moved to one place or another, while the trapeze lady, dressed in jeans and a sweater with holes in it, with her hair in curlers, smokes a "Chester" and walks off the tedium of the trip.

El Miko is busy helping several people move a trailer to one side when it shakes a bit and he hears a deep, angry growl from inside it. He steps back and a paw with claws idly sweeps out at him. He realizes he's been moving some lions around, his hand inches from the bars.

And now it's time to raise the tent.

The spikes are all sunk, the ropes positioned. It will take every hand there, young and old, to lift the tent top up the center pole. Taking command, a burly circus foreman walks around exhorting everyone to pull hard.

"Tíra! Tíra fuerte!"

El Miko pulls with the best of them and, meter by meter, the big tent moves up and up, rising like the excitement in every kids eyes. Up and up, further and further and at last it's there.

The tent is up. The trailers are all in place, forming a fence or barrier around the circus grounds. Tired but happy, *El Miko* is ready to get paid.

Suddenly, the friendly circus people aren't friendly anymore. Shouting angrily, the circus foreman chases out *El Miko* and the other nicely dressed foreign kids, pushing them past the barrier they have helped erect.

A few minutes later, clutching a measly few pesetas, the local Spanish kids are likewise ejected.

El Miko learns a lesson his 8 millimeter Kodak efforts like "The Scar" can't possibly teach him. It is his first job working with real professional show business people.

And they stiffed him.

14
Caminando

WE MIGHT HAVE GUESSED from early in our odyssey that going to Torremolinos will be like traveling into the past, because even just even getting there already is a clear step in that direction.

First, in a day when people routinely fly, we take an old-fashioned steamship across the Atlantic, a trip like something out of some historical movie, a 1958 version of "Titanic," minus Leonardo and Kate and the fatal iceberg.

And then, the bus ride up the coast from Algeciras is nothing at all like the clean modern buses I know in Chevy Chase, with hydraulic doors, smooth automatic transmissions, and steady, calm English speaking drivers stopping at well-marked bus stops.

No. The ancient bus we take up the coast would have looked good in a movie set in the 1930's, one of those migrants from the dust bowl dramas where a battered old bus full of destitute Okies wheezes and steams it's way across the prairies, looking for a better land to live in.

Our ride begins with the chaos of shouts and yells in Spanish as luggage is arranged and rearranged, and people pile on the whining, creaking, dusty old bus with doors pulled open and shut by hand. Each seemingly random stop seems to be the occasion for more shouting and commotion as this vehicle, grinding gears up and down all trip long, lurches and wheezes its way up the coast, bearing as much resemblance to the clean, modern buses of DC Transit as an antique biplane to a jet.

Apparently, in Spain, people don't get around the same modern way as they do in the States. To a child's eye this becomes more and more apparent with each day spent in Torremolinos when people took to *el camino,* they had some unusual, often dated, ways of going *caminando.*

Let's start with the cars.

We *Americanitos* are used to pretty much everybody having the usual USA suburban mix: big new Chevys, Fords, Chryslers, and lots of station wagons, the normal American humongo boatlike, gas guzzling sort of thing.

In Torremolinos big American cars are few and far between. Once in a blue moon somebody from one of the US military bases somewhere else in Spain drives one through, like a mammoth two-tone yacht floating down the narrow Spanish streets.

Instead there are all these oddly shaped cars, mostly older, with names that were foreign to Americans back then:

things like Peugeot, Volkswagen, Citroen, Mercedes and the Spanish SEATs, a licensed version of FIATs.

And these carmakers aren't going for big either. The operative word seems to be small, like to us practically go-kart small. These are like kid cars to us.

Plus, and this is the weirdest thing of all, most people here just don't have cars, period or, if they do, they have old ones. That's a shocker. Back in good old America it was a given that you not only had a car, but that every few years you traded it in for the shiny new model.

Here on Torremolinos, cars are far too expensive and *gasolina* costs far too much for the vast majority of local people to even dream of owning one.

Ni idéa. Don't even think about it.

When they can manage to scrap it together to get a new car, it' s a big event. Like when this retired *rejoneador* (that's a bullfighter who does his thing on horseback) in Torremolinos called Jose Maria Recondo manages to get a little SEAT 600. He proudly takes us kids and our mother for a ride down the coast.

It may well be his first car, because he's beaming with joy, probably out to impress the pretty *Americana*.

To us it's as weird as a Model T Ford: small, very small and cramped, kind of like one of the dinkiest of the Ford Metro's today, little more than a box on tiny wheels.

You squeeze into the diminutive seats inside it and, you're so low, you feel you're actually riding on the pavement as the tiny car howls and bumps wildly along the unevenly paved road, while the novice driver and bullfighter mercilessly grinds it's gears, jerking ineptly at the knob of the manual gear shift.

And he's one of the lucky few who could scrape enough *pesetas* together to buy even this tinny car. Most of

Torremolinos can't even dream of it. Coming from the US suburbia where owning a new car a given that's a new one for us.

So, without cars, how do people get around?

For starters, there are these weird wheezing old buses, locally called *Portillos* because a Mr. Portillo seems to have a monopoly on buses in our part of Málaga Province.

You take these up and down the coast and high up into the hills where the small mountain villages are.

One time we take this wheezing antique bus up to the mountain town of *Mijas* to see an Easter passion play and, on the way back, in the small village of *Arroyo de la Miel* (Spring of Honey), it slips into a ditch and smacks hard into the side of a building, sending the bus conductor, who's hanging out the open door, sprawling on the dirt road.

Other than cuts on his hand, nobody else on the overloaded bus is seriously hurt so, after a lot of chaos and shouting and confused running about, all the passengers get out and haul the bus out the ditch and we're on our gear-grinding way again, as if nothing at all has taken place.

That's the buses. Then there are the *motos.*

In our part of the USA back then, motorcycles are pretty much of a rarity, something you usually only see with a uniformed cop riding on it, leather boots, helmet and aviator shades on.

That whole Harley craze thing is way in the distant future, waiting for investment bankers and Malcom Forbes and movie stars and biker gangs that battle over turf.

But right now in Torremolinos *motos* are a big deal, they are more like cars are in America, because just about everyone can afford some form of two-wheeled motor driven thing.

And they truly run the gamut.

At the top of the *moto* food chain you find vehicles like the fancy BMW cycles the cops drive, with real transmission shafts instead of the usual chain drive. Also the pretty Spanish-made Montesa bikes with their distinctive red fuel tanks.

In some cases these are modified with short, downward pointing racing handlebars and leather padding on the fuel tank so the rider can hunch down and cut wind-resistance as he speeds along.

My Spanish friend Manolito introduces me to a guy called Santi who lives on the edge of town and rides one of these racing numbers in local races.

We see Santi roar along the carretera, hunched over the fuel tank, protected by racing leathers in case of a spill, and we think how cool that must be, flying like the wind on a howling Montesa that screams louder and sharper as you pop your way up the gears till you hit high gear and howl by whining furiously like some enraged fuel-guzzling metallic hornet.

Then, as you come halfway down the *moto* food chain, you find some smaller cheaper things?, the most noticeable of these is something called a *Guzzi*.

Guzzis look like they are hammered out of cheap tin, painted a sort of dull lifeless red. They have thinner tires, in-between a true motorcycle and a bike, and a smaller motor that pops high and continuously, like a gas-driven sewing machine that shakes the rear fender repeatedly when it isn't moving along the carretera.

The Guzzi sort of affords the look and the illusion of a true motorcycle for the many who can't actually afford the real thing.

There is one lower notch on the *moto* scale, saved for those who can't afford much in the way of a cycle and also as a sort of coming-of-age vehicle for local youths at age twelve, which was when you can legally drive these.

This is *la motocicleta* or motorbike.

By law your *motocicleta* has to have pedals, although with some models you can contrive to have these removed, perpetuating the illusion that it's actually a real *moto*, even though it isn't.

The reason a *motocicleta's* not the real thing is that it has to have a pretty small engine with a cylinder that's 49 cubic centimeters or less, so it's got little more than a lawn mower engine.

Still, with some models you can get a willing mechanic to sneak in a 65cc cylinder and get a little more in the way of road burning guts. But only a little.

As they hit twelve, all the Spanish kids I know get one.

Pacquito, whose parents own the small Hotel Flores, gets this black French thing called a Mobilete that has the engine mounted up front above the front tire, making it a bit ungainly and top heavy.

Manolito gets this grey-green Spanish-made thing called a Mosquito.

Perico, and his brother Armando have spiffy blue Ducatis. They are summertime kids from Sevilla whose family owns a huge house and garden off the main *carretera* just West of the Plaza Central.   Local boy Eduardo gets a red Derbi and promptly gives it the illegal 65cc head.

I want a *motocicleta* so bad, since it is sort of the badge of a young man back then, but my mother has other plans.

"You'll kill yourself on one of those. Over my dead body."

So I fantasize that my father, being a man, will somehow know to get me some kind of super cool miniature motorcycle, like a shrunken down version of the Bethesda cops' Harleys.

And that Xmas, there's a fairly heavy big cardboard box from him just for me.

Could it be? When I open it, my hopes soar as I spot a pair of metal handlebars with thick black rubber handgrips. I rip open the rest of the box feverishly, to unveil the rest of the motorcycle

And pull out a lousy pogo stick.

You could have just shot me right then and there.

That leaves me squarely at the bottom of the two-wheeled club with a lowly bicycle, something a lot of *Andaluzs* actually get by with because even a modest motorbike and the piddly gas bills it generates are too much for many people's incomes.

It's pretty normal to see local guys pedaling their bikes on Sunday along the highway with their girl friends or wives riding sidesaddle behind them, both all dressed up to go out to the movies or visit family or whatever.

Come the weekday there are tons of bicycle commuters, something foreign to someone from a culture where only kids ride bikes. At that pre-spandex bicycle pants time no self-respecting grownup tools around Chevy Chase on a bike, much less with their spouse sidesaddle on the back. They'd be the laughingstock of the neighborhood.

And there are many other more ancient forms of transportation around that leave Yankee kids wide-eyed as well.

Like for instance donkey carts. There are tons of them, pulled either by donkeys or larger mules or various combinations, sometimes two larger mules side by side with one smaller donkey up front to lead the way. A lot of stuff that's hauled around Torremolinos back then travels this way: bricks for buildings, beach sand to make cement with, the coal and wood for your cooking stove, the ice blocks, for your fridge, covered with straw mats and melting in the hot sun. All these things get around gracias to the clip-clopping hooves of these hard working creatures.

We even move house several times with all our belongings packed neatly into donkey carts.

You can ride them as well. Several times we hire small herds of donkeys and with young local guides make trips around the village and into the arid mountains. Mostly they just amble but when you give a donkey the right incentive, mainly a hard whack with a big stick, those little guys will really haul ass, no pun intended.

I see farmers do that around town, riding side saddle right over the rear haunches of their burros, steady as a rock as the little creatures gallop out of town towards the hills at a darn good clip.

The farmers urge their little steeds on with a long rolled "r" cry of *"Arrrrrrrrre muuula!"* or the more sonorous *"Soooooo booorrricaaaa!*

Up in the fields above the town, for plowing and for hauling really heavy jobs, there are teams of mammoth black or tan oxen standing higher than your head that slowly pull huge carts with wood wheels crudely fashioned from planks and bolted together.

The carts softly creak and groan, protesting their heavy loads, and move past you bit by bit as the gargantuan oxen plod by with huge hooves moving like they are underwater or caught on film and run in extremely slow motion.

I think the term "dumb as an ox" might have come about from the fact these big-eyed bovines move and react to commands as slowly as they do, like they exist in some other molasses dimension that's moving at a different, seriously ratcheted-down speed. It's like playing a 45 rpm disc at 33.

There are also, in this world of limited *pesetas* and expensive *gasolina*, all sorts of hybrid vehicles that you never see in the States.

Like true mini-trucks, so small they look kid-sized. Or three-wheeled motorcycle trucks, with flatbeds in the back and the driver up front on a motorcycle seat with handlebars.

Then there are the bubblecars, dinky two-seater things with a glass front that opens up as the door, two wheels in front, one in back. And there's the classic grey all corrugated tin *"Dos Caballos,"* the legendary two-horsepower French-made Citroen *deux Cheveaux* cars that putter like lawnmowers and lurch about wildly on unwieldy spring suspensions.

To a kid from the USA, all this is like you traveled through a time warp and landed on another planet where all the inhabitants moved about with a weird set of mysterious, weird science mobile contraptions.

And then there's *el tren*, the wonderful, magical train.

From the provincial capital of Málaga down the coast, through Torremolinos, and then on to Fuengirola, there's a noisy old steam engine that pulls, three or four times a day, six or seven old green wooden passenger cars with time-worn wooden seats.

The train is clearly from another era, a throwback time machine, maybe built in the forties or even thirties though it wouldn't look out of place racing over the Western Plains of America with war-whooping Indians on horseback in hot pursuit.

To us kids the train is totally cool.

Just the prospect of *el tren's* arrival at the old red brick and adobe station in the center of town somehow draws a crowd, particularly the last train at ten on a balmy summer evening.

Where the train tracks cross the *carretera* to Fuengirola, Elias' mustachioed, balding dad, in his blue railroad worker's slacks and grey shirt comes out of their railroad-owned house by the tracks and manually cranks down the barriers stopping traffic. That's his job and why they have that house.

Over where the tracks cross the *Calle San Miguel*, another railroad employee closes the flimsy red metal gates to stop cars and most pedestrians. You can still cross through some openings at the side and, as a kid, it seems your job to do that right up until the last moment when the train is about to run you down and your brother and sister yell at you to stop doing it or they'll tell Mom.

Before it arrives, you hear a distant whistle screaming in the night and a mighty chugging noise begins to grow and grow louder and louder as a single powerful light beam pierces the night. The whistle blasts again mightier and louder as the snarling roar of a heavy metal monster draws closer and begins to fill the summer night with its majestic thunder.

Then, with a blast of noise and billowing cloud of steam the train rushes through in a burst of deafening wind, belching a plume of black smoke and flaming sparks to the night sky as crowds hang on the gates and marvel at the very spectacle of it.

A few hundreds yards past the crossing, when it stops at the station, you walk through the crowds of dispersing travelers, smell the slightly burnt aroma of steam mixed with hot engine grease, and inspect the black steel engine itself, sitting there like some giant fire-breathing beast, stopping to catch its breath, before it rumbles off again into the night.

A few high whistles from the stationmaster, a blast of the mighty engine's own whistle, and it puffs off again, vanishing noisily into the blue-black Mediterranean evening.

You can also get your mom's permission and with your brother and friend Dana, ride the train on your own one day all the way to the end of the line to the beach town of Fuengirola, traveling part of the way outside on the open air platform at the end of each car.

When the steam train hurtles into the inky darkness of a tunnel, smoke and live cinders blow and billow all around you on the open platform as you hold on the rails and scream for joy amid all the beautiful roar of steam engine noise.

On the way back the train gets crowded and Mark and I watch in fascination and stunned surprise as we realize one guy in the packed train is a pickpocket.

We don't know much Spanish at this point and aren't at all sure if it is safe to speak up so we just watch wide-eyed as the pickpocket's hand slithers out from a newspaper he is holding and undulates gracefully like a sinuous serpent across another man's chest and into the breast pocket of his suit coat.

A moment later the hand snakes silently back, clutching the victim's worn brown leather wallet which the pickpocket surreptitiously slips to a small boy, younger than us, innocently standing next to him.

Then they are gone in the crowd, off to the next rail car and the next victim.

Back at the Torremolinos station, again admiring the puffing behemoth, you see the engineer greet an ancient beret-clad *campesino* leading his burro, a man so old he cups his hand to his ear to aid his faint hearing.

As is customary, they say hello by saying goodbye.

"*Adiós, Tomás,*: says the engineer, "*Qué le vaya bien.*"

"*Si, adiós, muchacho,*" comes the reply.

The old man lifts his black armband-clad arm and holds up to his lips a toothpick, speared in it the inch-long remains of a lit cigarette. He takes a last puff or two of his precious *cigarillo.*

Then he bends down between the rails to pick up a few pieces of unburnt coal the train has dropped, and adds it to the stash of coal already in his burro's basket.

That's apparently how the old man Tomás gets the money to buy those *cigarillos*, he trades or sell lumps of coal he scavenges from the railroad tracks.

The cigarette vendor at the station is a young boy, no older than me, with a homemade cardboard tray full of cigarettes you can buy one by one or, if you only have a little money, he will cut them with a razor blade and sell you half a *cigarillo*.

Besides the cheap Spanish *Celta* and *Ducado* cigarettes he sells plenty of American brands you can ask for with its own Spanishized garbled up American name.

Winstons. *"Weenstones."*

Marlboros. *"Maroburros."*

Chesterfields. *"Chesters."*

Lucky Strikes. *"Lookies."*

Taking a last puff of his cigarette on a toothpick, the old man smiles at me and waves an *adios*. Then he walks off leading his old burro by its old woven hemp halter. With his beat up beret and walking stick, he seems a classic image of village life as it probably has existed undisturbed for centuries.

But the world is in fact changing. The idea that an *americano* like me is even there to see all of this is a sign that all manner of new things are on the way.

Like the diesel.

One day, Manolito tells me the steam engine won't be coming through town anymore. In order to better move the growing number of tourists around, they've replaced it with something brand spanking new he calls *El Dee-esel*, the diesel.

We go down to the train crossing the first evening to see this marvelous new modern invention. As before, the railway guard lowers the red gates, the crowd gathers, the same air of excitement builds in the balmy night air: the train is coming!

But now instead of the high shrieking whistle, percussive chugging and the majestic rolling thunder of the steam engine, we hear something far less dramatic:

A single very high-pitched horn, sounds weakly in the distance like some diminutive electronic sheep or the warning buzzer on an elevator door.

Two feeble headlights shine dimly through the night and, instead of the heroic chug and massive roaring bluster of a steam engine, you barely hear anything at all except the monotonous clicking of steel wheels on the rails.

Something resembling two large green and cream buses slides unremarkably by on the rails, making a small clicketing sound. This *"dee-esel"* as the villagers call it isn't just faster, roomier and more modern than the old steam engine.

It's almost silent. And it's swifter.

That is great for all the impatient tourists who want to get everywhere faster on their vacations.

But not for the old coal scavenger guy.

The old man is a kilometer east of town bending down as usual to look for pieces of coal between the rails, his burro waiting patiently beside him, nibbling on the grass by the rails.

Suddenly, the donkey looks up from the grass and brays. The old man yells: *"Quieto"* to be quiet but it pulls at its halter and backs away from the rails.

The half deaf old *campesino* smiles, shakes his head, and bends back down looking for those precious pieces of coal that pay for his *cigarillos.*

In a few heartbeats, the steel and chrome train silently comes hurtling around the corner, a bright and shiny, new diesel-powered future headed bang on a collision course with the unsuspecting raggedy old past.

Blam!

It hurls the frail old man several hundred meters. They say he was probably dead well before his broken old body smashed down and went flailing and rolling on the ground.

The news shoots around town in an instant and all the kids know about it in a flash. The *"dee-esel"* has killed *"el viejo Tomás"* and they put his banged up and bloody dead body in one of the new train's cars at the station.

There's no question about it, you have to run down there and, waiting your turn, push through the crowd of kids to look inside.

You perch on the doorstep of the train, press your nose hard to the cool glass of the window, straining to look down at the motionless figure lying all twisted, bloodied and broken on the floor inside.

They say progress has a way of burying everything that came before it.

Pressed tight against the train door window I look down and see that it does indeed.

I am sick to my stomach for the rest of the day.

I can't stop seeing the crumpled corpse of the past, head split open, battered and bloody and covered with hungry, mean-looking flies with iridescent green eyes.

Torremolinos

David M. Johnson

15
"El Terremoto"

TORREMOLINOS IS JUST BARELY BIG
ENOUGH in the late 1950s to warrant two rival *carniceros*,
or butcher shops, both them named Martín (pronounced "Mar-
teen") owned I think by cousins.

The first Martiín butcher near the top of *Called San
Miguel* on the east side of the street, the other is further down
on the west side, almost to the *Bar Quitapenas* where the heavy

213

drinkers hang out every lunch time getting stewed on *Málaga Dulce* or some local *tinto*.

Each of these two competing butcher owners has a son, both in their early twenties. Like all self-respecting young village men of means at that time, they, of course, have motorcycles, and do deliveries for their respective butcher dads. They are probably rivals, not just in the art of slogging meat around, but for the affections of the young women of the village as well.

And these *señoritas* probably don't fail to notice, as does the town, that both *carniceros* sons are quite different.

Emilio, the son from the east side of the street butcher is kind of quiet. He talks softly and, while he sports the requisite young gun's sunglasses, still seems to me a touch of what we now call a nerd.

There is just something a little uncoordinated about him, but he seems like a nice guy. Not surprisingly, he is *un estudiante* at a university in Málaga when he isn't delivering steaks, pork chops, cut up chickens and the rest.

Baldomero, the west side of the street butcher's dude, now he is a whole other kind of animal.

He wears aviator shades quite rakishly. He has a fast looking, red Montesa bike with those short kind of racing handlebars, and he just sort of sits on it, arms folded, carefully combing his brown, not quite *"rubio"* locks. His head is held up high and cocked to one side with this whole pose that just says it all.

"I am cool. Dig me."

I'm not sure whether I like him or not, but you can't fail to notice his act.

And maybe it isn't just an act.

When it comes time to show you've got guts, Baldomero seems to be front and center.

I see him fly his motorcycle down the steep curved hill towards the *Carihuela,* doing maybe fifty or so, blond hair waving in the slipstream, wrapped white paper sack of meat resting on top of the Montesa's gas tank, and hands folded across this chest, nowhere near the handlebars.

"Look, ma, no hands," at fifty an hour puts Baldomero in the *cojones* club for me.

I also remember him at a spring village *fiesta* at night where they hang a small ring on a ribbon from a wire across *Calle San Miguel* and the young lads take turns racing their motorcycles down the street,

Inches from the crowd on either side, they gun their cycles by trying to snag the ring with a small stick, while still going fast enough to not be called a chicken.

Baldomero not only drives his bike the fastest, weaving dangerously near the spectators, but damn if he isn't the one to snag the ring.

He follows that up by repeatedly jumping his bike over the huge bonfire set in the middle of the street. Aviator shades still on, of course.

I don't know how Emilio, the quiet butcher's son, feels about all that but I bet there is one thing he dislikes about his rival: Baldomero has snagged, as well as the ring, Sabiliche.

Sabiliche is maybe sixteen or so and works at a local hairdressers. She has long black hair, beautiful dark eyes and slightly olive skin. Plus an awesome figure.

Nobody uses the term "hot" back then, but believe me she is *muy caliente.*

Conjure up your best image of a sexy Spanish *señorita,* play a little flamenco in your head, make her dance seductively with some castanettes and you might be halfway there if you're lucky.

She is also a truly nice young lady. I know for a fact because she talks to us kids all quite easily with friendly smile for everyone. I remember having a sort of crush on her.

But, of course, she is Baldomero's girl and, hey, I'm just a kid.

So somehow, between the aviator shades, the fast motorcycle, the derring do and, of course, Sabiliche, I begin to wonder if Baldomero isn't someone to pattern yourself after, someone a little kid should emulate.

I mean, Davy Crockett is rapidly fading into my misty past and Torremolinos is becoming my here and now. Is Baldomero the guy I should try to be, trade in my coonskin cap for a pair of rakish aviator shades?

I begin to picture myself with those sunglasses perched nonchalantly on my head, astride a racy red Montesa. Just trying it on for size. Maybe Sabeliche's on the back seat, arms wrapped tight around me.

So, at least in my young mind, I am beginning to put the great sons of the *carniceros* rivalry to rest. Baldomero wins.

That's when Torremolinos figures out how to elevate the contest to the most Spanish of levels: a bullfight arena.

It is decided both young men will learn the art of bullfighting and will then duel *mano a mano,* man to man, in a real *corrida*, a bullfight with dangerous sharp-horned bulls.

This is major news that sets the whole village talking.

Will they go through with it? Will the student e*l estudiante* finally best Baldomero? Will the later really have enough *cojones* to face the sharp horns of a charging *novillo*?

This is cool. And, as a local kid, I get to see some of the preparations. Like watching this retired bullfighter called Antonio Maria Recondo teach them both the passes with the large *capote*, or cape, while a young boy pushing a wheel barrow outfitted with horns plays the role of the charging bull.

Some of us kids even get to try our hand at it with this harmless one-wheeled bull trying to gore us.

To this day I can still show you how to *citar* , or address, the bull with one hand held forward, giving the cape a sharp tug to get the dangerous beast's attention. Then, as he charges, intent on goring you to death, plant your foot and swing the cape, hopefully drawing the hurtling animal past you.

Then repeat that to the other side and again and so on until the bull is momentarily tired and befuddled, at which point you bravely sign it all off by twirling your cape in a snazzy pin-wheeling *rebolera* and turn your back to the bull to receive the thunderous applause and admiration of the crowd and the smiling Sabiliche.

At least, that's how it is in my boyish dreams.

I also see Baldomero get training only a *carnicero* can get: practicing how to kill a bull by actually killing a cow in his father's slaughterhouse with the tools of the bullfighter's trade, a sharp *espada*, or sword, and, should that fail to do the job, a *descabello* sword with a sideways blade to quickly sever the thrashing beast's spinal chord.

This will definitely not pass muster with the animal rights people of the future, but this is another time and place.

Some Spanish friends and I brave the harsh mid-day sun, traipsing up to the *Calvario* section on the mountainside, to peak into the cool and dark interior of the slaughterhouse. It's really just a large whitewashed wall barn where Baldomero has come to learn the kind of quick, clean kill that will earn him an ear or more in the corrida.

As far as we can see, he doesn't get the idea really well, as the poor cow is standing there quite some time waiting to be dispatched, enduring sword thrust after sword thrust and then, after about four tries with the *descabello* sword, finally dying, probably out of boredom more than anything else.

It doesn't look to us like Baldomero is going to earn any ears for his killing technique. But, just before the bullfight, he more than makes up for any shortcomings there with a *torero's* nickname that fits his flamboyant personality:

Baldomero Martín: "*El Terremoto*"

"The Earthquake."

The notion that the very earth should shake at his command is every bit as unassuming and modest as the young *carnicero* himself.

But it makes a little American kid wonder: maybe with chutzpah like that, he actually might make a real *torero*.

And so, much of the village of Torremolinos finds itself some time later in a small wooden bullring, trucked in and set up in the mountain town of Churriana, ready to view the *mano a mano* of all *mano a manos*: Emilio *"El Estudiante"* The Student, versus "*El Terremoto*" The Earthquake.

I can't remember much of Emilio's performance.

I think he fights the first bull and is fairly creditable. He looks a little scared but goes out anyhow and does a decent job and, while his killing technique leaves something to be desired, he certainly has an edge over "*El Terremoto's*" slaughterhouse performance.

I believe he earns a couple of ears and some good applause.

Then it is time for "The Earthquake."

His *cuadrilla,* professional *toreros* who know the drill and are hired to be Baldomeros protector's and assistants, go to unlatch the door to release the waiting bull into the ring.

But they are stopped by a loud shout from Baldomero.

The butcher's bold son, chest puffed out, strides to an area 10 meters in front of the door, waving the *cuadrilla* away with a dramatic gesture.

He flings his cape around on the sand, and gets on his knees to face the bull as it enters, arms spread out in a defiantly welcoming gesture preparing to, at the last minute, swirl the cape and deflect the bull's murderous initial charge.

There follow some shouts from his contingent cautioning him against this foolish move as he is about to face a charging bull, on his knees, without a cape held out between him and the bull.

They try to reason with the inexperienced young bullfighter, to tell him this is not at all the thing to do, it is sheer folly.

Baldomero shakes his head, will have none of it. He waves them histrionically away and shouts, head held high, to have them release the angry bull.

"The Earthquake" has spoken.

He will face the bull alone on his knees in the sand.

Reluctantly, the assistants shake their heads and unlatch the door to let out the ferocious beast.

They swing it open.

The bull runs straight out like a shot.

And it tramples "*El Terremoto*" into the very earth he is supposed to be shaking, not eating.

Then it tears off around the ring looking for something more challenging to gore, leaving Baldomero motionless and crumpled in the sand.

In a flurry of capes and shouting, the men of his cuadrilla distract the bull while some lift the dazed Baldomero and start to drag him to safety, perhaps even to an ambulance.

Recovering his senses, Baldomero shakes them off and, with an angry shout strides over to confront the bull, again capeless, and screaming at it in outrage, his chest puffed out and arms held high in anger, as if to say how in the heavens would it dare to challenge him.

Hearing his shouts, the beast turns and charges him and again it knocks him right over and then runs on to more interesting things, while his cuadrilla leaps into action again, picking him out of the dusty sand, only to have him shake them off again.

That's pretty much how the fight goes, with the bull knocking Baldomero down repeatedly, only to have him bob back like one of those inflatable clowns you punch down that pop up again.

He pops up, does a pass or two, makes some other foolish move in front of the bull, then gets blasted back down.

How he keeps from getting gored I don't know.

But his once pristine *traje de luces*, or "suit of lights", is ripped open in several places, covered with arena sand, showing his white underwear.

And his usually perfectly-combed wavy hair is mussed up and sticking out haphazardly in crazy angles.

He looks less like a noble bullfighter than he does some tattered rodeo clown. Or a buffoon in a circus.

Then it is time for the moment of truth.

This is the obligatory clean kill he has rehearsed on the slaughterhouse cows, the true mark of a *matador* (which by the way means "killer").

Well, friends, he may just as well be right back in the slaughterhouse because he has not got a whit better. It just goes on and on, stab after hopeless stab, until you find yourself begging that the bull will just somehow die of old age or be struck by lightning or something, please, God.

Even though it seems to take forever, when the bull is finally dispatched, the crowd goes bananas over Baldomero's performance, as if he had actually done something, even one thing, right.

They wave so many white handkerchiefs that "*El Terremoto*" is awarded both ears, the tail and a hoof. It has to be for sheer guts because his performance wouldn't earn one hair from the bull in any real *corrida*.

The most amazing thing of all is that despite what has to be considered a very clownish performance Baldomero goes on to pursue for awhile a career as a *torero*, gaining some fans here and there.

There is even a popular song written in his honor *"Baldomero Martín: El Terremoto."*

"The Earthquake."

He even manages to be formally presented in the hallowed Madrid bullring of Las Ventas in 1962 displaying "a coarse bullfighting style" that is savaged by "the critics of the day who mercilessly condemned his performance," according to an online Malaga tourism site.

Despite that, Baldomero fights on, the site reports, to graduate to full matador status in an *alternativa* blessed by rockstar matador *El Cordobes*. Once again, the site says "he was similarly unimpressive.....as a result he decided not to perform again."

Not surprised.

Because that afternoon of his very first fight ever the earth did not shake for me.

There was no *terremoto.*

And I realized that Baldomero to me was no longer someone to emulate, but a solid example of everything to avoid.

Even as an *americanito* I have by now seen enough bullfights to know how it is supposed to go down.

It's a ballet, it has grace and dance-like moves.

Bullfighting is like an art form where, with every performance, death is in the house. Not the bull's death, because that's a foregone conclusion, but the very real possibility of one of the *toreros* dying on a bull's horns.

Those beasts can kill you. And they are bred to want that very much.

The proper thing for you to do in the ring, in the face of this panting and malevolent, hooved death, is not to act the clown. But to be every inch the man.

By now I'd seen that in the legendary *mano a manos* of Luis Miguel Dominguin and Antonio Ordonez, two demigods of the ring, and in the quiet grace and beauty of Paco Camino who, some years later in Bailen, died on the horns of a bull called Camacho.

Paco has what it takes.

According to Ernest Hemingway that means a great *matador* needs three special things: "Courage, skill in his profession and grace in the presence of the danger of death."

Baldomero has shown neither of the latter two, as "skill" and "grace" describe to me absolutely nothing he has done.

And as for courage, I'm beginning to doubt that's what "El Terremoto" brings to the party.

Like I said, death is in the house.

Only, that steamy hot afternoon in the wooden ring in Churriana, the only thing that dies for me is the illusion that Baldomero is the way he is because he has a lot of guts and is someone to emulate.

I decide he is either just plain crazy.

Or stupid.

Or both.

Torremolinos

David M. Johnson

16
Moises

WHEN OTHER KIDS IN TORREMOLINOS
ask me, as they often do in the normal course of children's
inquiries about each other, why we the Johnson's from Chevy

Chase, Maryland, have chosen to live in Spain, I'm always at a loss to come up with any reasonable explanation.

Think it through.

My father hasn't been stationed here with the military or the diplomatic corps; in fact he doesn't even live with us. So that pretty clearly rules those out.

And my mother doesn't have one of those fancy jobs with some big U.S. corporation.

After rejecting all those lines of questioning, often the puzzled friend smiles and all by themselves arrives at the one truly obvious solution.

"It's because you're of Spanish descent."

Now this is a handy explanation that, in one fell swoop, solves the entire mystery quite satisfactorily.

But sorry, Charlie or Carlos or whatever.

I'm a lot of different things: Welsh, Dutch, French and even German, But not a drop of Spanish blood courses through this Gringo's veins.

Despite that inconvenient fact, I have to admit our little family eventually does have one full-fledged Spanish member. And he's a true native of Torremolinos itself: Moises or *El Mosey*.

Our *perrito español*: our little Spanish dog.

Here's why that's so.

One day, my brother Mark is walking along the dusty dirt path by the railroad tracks that lead east out of town towards Málaga. He's a few hundred yards out of town, just past the gleaming pink concrete jewel of the *Cine Universal,* where the white-washed, red-tiled roof houses give way to farmed fields and small, foot-wide irrigation ditches often filled with gurgling water.

Suddenly *"El Miko"* hears an unusual and small little sound. It's a tiny whimpering cry, kind of like the mewing of a newborn kitten. Curious, he looks down along the irrigation ditch where it leads into a field of sugar cane, and makes a tiny discovery.

It's a little black, newborn something, so newly arrived in this world it's still wet from its mother's insides. It's so tiny and curled up that, when Mark tucks it into his shirt and brings it home, it's hard to tell if we are presented with a baby kitten or perhaps even some kind of rodent, with it's eyes all shut and tiny feet tucked into a small furry body.

My mother inspects it and quickly informs us of several things. First, it's a dog, a little baby boy dog. And second, it will not likely live more than a day: it's been separated far too early from its mother, which she surmises might be a young bitch so surprised at having a litter that she dropped the first baby dog by some running water and ran for safer haven with the rest of the puppies yet to come.

"*La Señora* is certainly right, he will die," our maid says taking one cursory look at the doomed little creature.

"Can we keep him and feed him? Maybe he'll live, you'll see, please, Mommy," we reply, oblivious to life's harsher realities.

Kids simply don't believe in death, certainly not of one of their own, another kid, some poor dog lady's first child.

So we set about to save the little creature. My sister, "*La Mimi*", runs around the corner to the two little old ladies in black who sell candy from their modest home. She had noticed, among their wares, small little baby bottles filled with little round and colored sugar candies, and topped with tiny rubber nipples, and Mimi brings one of these back.

We unceremoniously dump the candy, poke a hole in the nipple, fill the bottle with warm milk and attempt to feed the little creature, as if he were our very own diminutive baby brother.

He weakly sucks at the nipple and milk spills out on him and on us and it's hard to tell if he is getting any at all.

After a while, and another bottle or two of our candy baby bottle milk go all over the place, his struggles to suck grow fainter and eventually cease all together, and he stops moving.

Quietly, we wrap him in a blanket, put him in a cardboard box in the bedroom I share with Mark, and, as it is late evening, retire for the night, with our mother's warning not to have our hopes too high that the little thing will still be alive the next morning.

When the rising Mediterranean sun wakes us, we cautiously peer into the box. The little black thing lies motionless in his white blanket, without making a sound. Sure of the worst, my brother gently picks the likely dead puppy up and discovers something:

The pup is warm to the touch and makes a few struggling little motions and a tiny cry comes out of his little pink mouth.

He isn't just alive, he's wondering where the heck that little baby bottle is, because he's ravenous, sucking away hard at our fingers. I think this is when we know that, as small as he is, he's going to make it.

And our family has a new member, the first and only real honest to god Spanish relative we can ever claim.

We dub him Moses, in Spanish *Moises*, because he was born near the water, if not by actual bullrushes, in the long weeds that grow by the irrigation channel.

And Moses, like the baby from the Bible, thrives.

He quickly graduates from the candy-sized baby bottle to the real thing, a full-size baby bottle our mother buys at an *almacen* in town.

Then he progresses to plates of bread mushed up in warm milk, which he gobbles up greedily in such large quantities his stomach swells up and he rolls over on his back by the dish, tiny paws in the air. Stuffed, he groans in bloated delirium, his huge pink belly swelled up like he's one of those middle-aged tourists you see at the beach, with their humongous stomachs thrust out to the world, like those of extremely pregnant ladies.

He just lies there on his back grinning, stuffed to the exploding point, and moaning:

"Uhnnnnnnnnnnnnnnnnnn-uh!"

"Uhnnnnnnnnnnnnnnnnnn-uh!"

As he grows and takes on a more definite shape than the roly poly outlines of a pup, we can see he's a bird dog: small, about thirty-five pounds, with the stance and gait of a true pointer.

He's in the family area that includes Weimeraners, Vizlas, and German short- haired pointers, only smaller and black with white markings on his chest and paws.

When people on the street see us walk him, they like his look and often inquire what breed he is. My mother cleverly invents a new class of canine: the "Andalusian Retriever," and that's what we tell all who ask.

They usually nod and go away happy having learned about this new and wonderful breed from Andalusia, the South of Spain.

Children and dogs are a match made in heaven, and that's where we are, in kid paradise, having Moses, or Mosey, as a pal and confidant and plaything. He's the newest Johnson and something we fight over and enjoy as if he were the shiniest new Christmas toy.

We laugh and chase him all over the house, then turn around and run like mad, laughing hysterically, while he chases us, his feet scrabbling as his nails slip and slide on the cool Spanish tile floors.

We play the same game at the beach, laughing as Mosey runs on the beach and slips trying to make turns in the soft sand, then we run screaming into the water where he swims valiantly after us, little black head held high out of the waves as his feet churn madly.

Once, when he's still small, we came back from a local *feria and* feel sorry that he hasn't been able to enjoy the carnival rides like us. So we devise one with a woven basket and a rope.

In the straw basket goes Moses and then around and around as Mark swings the rope, then for a grand finale, Moses gets to do loop the loops, swinging high over Mark's head, then swooping down to just skim the floor.

Fortunately, he survives our carnival ride, though he blows his milk and bread lunch all over the floor after woozily staggering from the basket. We just want him to have the same fun we've been having, to be a real people.

And that's what Mosey thinks he is, a people.

Think about it. He's never even known his dog mama, or brothers and sisters, never tasted an ounce of real dog's milk, he's raised from the get go by humans.

They say that baby ducks at a certain point will accept whatever they see as their mother, if the same is true for dogs, Mosey must be convinced that his mama is a human, and by logical canine deduction so is he.

Consequently he's never very interested in other dogs, doesn't like sniffing them, or vice versa, and basically ignores them as some lower creature that humans like him needn't really bother themselves with.

He's a Johnson, a people, not some four-legged butt-sniffing hairy hooligan.

No, sir.

He wants to hang with us and do whatever we do. We even learn we could make him howl wildly like a wolf if we sit together and howl first. He sees us in action, throws his head back, makes a perfect little circle with his mouth and howls like a wild timberwolf.

This idea that he's a people seems to bother him when it comes time to bed down for the night. We all have proper beds which my mother rules are strictly off limits to Mosey, while all he has is a sleeping basket with a blanket, hardly the right sort of place for a human being like him to sack out.

For shame! *Que verguenza*!

In all the years he lives, he never stops trying to sneak into our beds, and he gets so good at doing it by stealth, you often wake up in the morning to find him there, with no recollection of Moses ever climbing in.

He has a great technique for doing it, one we are all able to admire over time. Moses bides his time, waiting for the whole household to be sound asleep. Then he creeps silently to the chosen bed, and stands there silently for easily twenty minutes, making sure his intended victim is off in dream world and fast asleep.

If you aren't asleep, you have to pretend you are to fully appreciate his cunning technique.

After the patient dog studies you sleeping for a long while, you feel the lightest plonk on the bed as he places one paw lightly on it.

Then he waits for any reaction, to see if you even stir. He stays like this a good ten minutes, just to be sure, one paw on the bed, his gaze fixed on the sleeping victim.

Then another light plonk, another paw, and another ten minutes holding his breath to make sure he hasn't roused you.

In this slow, silent fashion, he paw-by-paw climbs into bed with you without waking you up.

He even manages to miraculously part the blanket, like the biblical Moses parted the Red Sea, so he can climb under it and snuggle in underneath it.

The whole process takes close to an hour, and if you wake or stir he slinks sneakily away to a dark corner, then comes back later when he's convinced you're again asleep, driven by his relentless desire to sleep in a proper bed like a real human being.

Another side effect of his rather unorthodox upbringing is Mose's sick foot fetish.

It almost certainly comes about from his living as a pup on the floor in a box. Down there, the first sight he sees before being fed or loved is the shoe of the human who's come up to him. He must somehow connect love and shoes deep in his psyche.

This canine foot fixation is so intensely ingrained in his subconscious that you can't come over to our house and cross your legs, extending one foot out, because that's like a red flag to a bull with Mosey.

He's over in a flash and, rather than simply humping your leg like an ordinary common dog might do, he just slowly rubs his doggy weiner on your foot, back and forth, with this disgustingly cheesy look on his face, like some perverted old guy looking at dirty magazines in a sleazy X-rated bookstore.

It's so sick yet inevitable that any guest at our house has no choice but to keep their feet down or risk the assault of the Great Four-Legged Spanish Foot Pervert, *Moises*

Moses is the most authentic piece of Torremolinos we have in our house, born and bred here from local stock.

He's the only true Spaniard in our family, and he carries himself about the village with a proud walk, much like a true

Andalusian *señor* might proudly ride by on his horse, head held high in the air.

One time in particular, I see him get his comeuppance for donning such foolishly lofty airs.

I'm walking with him to the beach through the cobblestone and dusty dirt streets of the *Bahondillo* fishing village in the mid morning sun. The day is already heating up.

Up ahead, on the top of the two stone steps leading into some local fisherman's white-washed modest house, lays a large calico fishing village cat, basking in the sweet rays of Southern Spanish sun.

In a rough and tumble fishing village, these are not exactly pussycats

Perhaps offended that this cat doesn't get up and pay his respects by giving Moses a wide berth, our insulted dog barks furiously at the cat and makes a half run at him to teach the little pussycat a lesson

Barely ruffled, the cat opens one sleepy eye, yawns lazily. stretching a leg out to and flexing its claws, and just looks with absolute indifference at Moses standing there with his chest puffed out and head high in the air.

Further enraged by this lack of proper respect to his exalted personage, angry Moses again barks and starts another courageous run at the stone steps and the feline enemy.

The cat doesn't move a muscle, just sleepily watches Moses approach flaunting his canine snarling bluster.

Then there's a blur.

And the cat springs fast like a bolt of lightning off the steps and perches right on top of Moses' black back, a feline horseman mounting his trusty canine steed.

With a firm motion, the cat digs its claws deep into the startled dog's tender flesh to get a better grip and perhaps to signal a "giddyup!".

Mose's eyes bulge wide, he yelps in pain, and he runs around the street in three rapid circles, the cat astride him like some trick rider in the circus.

As the third circle draws near the stone steps, the cat jumps nimbly off to the same spot where it had been happily sleeping, like the guy who runs the carousel at an amusement park steps off nimbly and exactly at the control wheel after taking your ticket.

Yelping in more fear and surprise than pain, Mosey takes off like a shot for home where we find him later cowering under a bed, with a few bloody cat claw marks to show for his arrogance and miscalculation.

On the steps of the fisherman's house, without even a glance at the fleeing Moses, the cat yawns, daintily licks some dog hair off a paw, and goes lazily back to sleep in the sun.

Despite all his local blood and his lofty pedigree as a bonfide "Andalusian Retriever" and a son of this village, Moses learns a little lesson that day about the pecking order in Torremolinos and who sits at the top of it.

Obviously, any cat tough enough to stay alive and prosper in a tough hardscrabble dirt poor fishing village, where people can barely afford shoes, is not a candidate for the phrase "pussycat".

That's one Spanish lesson Moses never forgets, for I never see him even bark even meekly at any sort of cat again.

He will, however, keep his pedigree as a 100% Spaniard pure by living his entire life in Spain, never setting foot on real American soil, unless you count the few times he went to the vet at Torrejon Air Force Base outside of Madrid where my mother worked long after we'd all returned to the U.S. for college.

Maybe we puzzled kids never could thoroughly explain why we were in Spain in the first place but at least one four-legged member of our family always had an ironclad excuse.

"*Hombre, porque soy espanol.*"

"Dude, I'm Spanish."

Lagartijo

17
Los toros

"AGUA! AGUA! AGUA!"

Baked by the relentless afternoon Málaga sun, the bullfight arena crowd is chanting for cooling water in the cheap seats, the *sol* section, so named for the glaring hot summer *sol* high in the sky that is roasting alive the bullfight fans in their section, like so many basted chickens turning over the fire at a Spanish country barbecue.

Out on the golden-orange sands of the bullring the objects of the crowds' chant ignore them and do their assigned job. Two fat *bomberos*, Málaga firemen, wield equally fat hoses on either side of their red tank truck, waving them back and forth to wet down the dry sands before the start of the *corrida*.

I've seen the groundsmen do sort of the same thing with the ballpark infield at Griffith Park in D.C., before a Washington Senators game with the New York Yankees, back when superstar Mickey Mantle was on the legendary team.

Only here in Málaga, the great national past time isn't baseball. It's *los toros*, the bullfights.

It's a tradition that goes back centuries with a shining pantheon of hallowed heroes whose names echo through time: Manolete, Lagartijo, Romero, Belmonte.

Today, in the cheap sun-baked seats the sweltering crowd begins to chant even louder, begging for relief from the heat.

"Agua!!! Agua!!! Agua!!!"

With a smile and a shrug at each other, the *bomberos* relent.

In unison, they wave their hoses high above the crowd in the *sol* section and send a few quick mini rain showers onto the sweltering crowd. People shout in delight: a few women squeal and cover themselves with their arms, but most just raise their faces to receive the cool and welcome relief from the sky.

The *bomberos* pack their hoses quickly into their fire truck and drive off in a gruff snort of diesel fumes.

In our mercifully already shaded seats in *sol y sombra*, the sun and shade section, we check the president's box high in the most expensive *sombra*, or shade, section.

All the important officials are there, the *corrida* will soon begin, right on time as we know it will.

You see, this may be a Spain where very little runs on time. A five o'clock bus may show up at five thirty or six, a ten a.m. business appointment may actually be honored at twelve; a firm Wednesday arrangement can easily take place on Thursday.

But *los toros*, you can set your watch by.

If the colorful bullfight posters say *la corrida* will go on at *"las cinco de la tarde,"* you can bet your family fortune that at five in the afternoon precisely, en *punto*, it will commence.

Today is no exception.

And, at least on these pages, you're here sitting next to me. Enjoy your first *corrida.*

The second the clock hits five, the brass band in the nosebleed seats strikes up and, as a red gate is opened at the far end, the *alguacil* rides in on a proudly prancing Andalusian stallion.

Dressed in black seventeenth century robes, the *alguacil* rides over to the sands beneath the president's box, and doffs his feathered hat, asking for permission to hold this *corrida*.

This formality granted, he trots his steed back to the gate to lead the opening procession.

As the band launches into a timeless *pasodoble*, he turns his horse and leads all the players in.

First, the *matadors*, or killers, the guys who do the center stage work with the bull and, in the end, actually dispatch it. To *matar* is to kill and these guys are the pros at it.

They always get star billing on the posters and the good *matadors* get salaries to go with it. The very top ones are millionaires and in Spain are treated like Hollywood gods or rock stars. In most bullfights there are three, today it's a *mano a mano*, a face-off, and there are just two.

But not just any two.

These guys are flesh and blood Spanish superheroes.

On the left, a real living legend, and the one with the most years performing on the bloody sands: Luis Miguel Dominguin.

Luis Miguel was on the bill and in the ring the day the legendary Manolete was gored to death in Linares. Back then, Dominguin was the new young Turk on the block, maybe even the reason Manolete went out of his way, a little too far as luck would have it, with a bull called Islero to prove to the crowd that the old man still had it.

Today Luis Miguel is a multi-millionaire pal of Ernest Hemingway and a one-time lover of movie star Ava Gardner.

And on the right is today's new young Turk who now challenges the old pro (what goes around comes around): Antonio Ordoñez.

Antonio only just became a full-fledged matador more than four years after Dominguin shared the ring with the ill-fated Manolete. But now Ordoñez is the guy many whisper is the best today, as they murmur that Dominguin's star is fading with each passing year, the older man is slowing down and no longer has it.

Each man is here in the ring today to prove that they, and not the other guy, are the real *número uno*, and to put all the arguments and counter arguments and whispers to rest: with artistry, bravery and the blood of the bulls.

Between them, in their separate careers, these *matadors* have already killed, 6,027 bulls, winning 5,023 ears and 657 tails in the process.

After today's six bulls, the ear and tail tally may finally prove, in bloody trophies, who is greatest *matador* of the day.

Together, the two rivals stride in, proud and resplendent in their gold-embroidered *trajes de luces*, or suits of lights, so called for the way the sun kicks sparkles of light off the sequins on their costumes.

Below their knee-length matador pants they wear pink stockings and soft black *zapatillas* or leather shoes that wouldn't look out of place on a ballet stage (only nobody dies when they perform "Swan Lake").

On their heads, each bullfighter wears the black, sort of monkey-eared *montera* that replaced the three-corner hat as matador wear in the nineteenth century.

Behind these two veritable megastars of the sands, come their *cuadrillas*, the guys in their employ who help them evaluate the bull, set various stages of the fight up for them, and swiftly come to their rescue if they get in mortal peril.

The *cuadrilla* members wear costumes similar to the matadors, just as not as bright and flashy (you don't want to upstage the boss).

The matador's life is quite often literally in the hands of his cape-bearing *cuadrilla*. He chooses them very carefully. You would, too.

Next come the big fat *picadors*, beefy mean-looking thugs with fifteen foot lances, riding bony nags, horses wearing creamy-yellow full length pads down their right flanks and fronts.

Nobody in the crowd likes the *picadors*, they're like the bad guys at a wrestling match, but they're here because they've got a job to do.

At the tail end of the procession, there are a bunch of *monosabios,* or "wise monkeys", in blue work pants and red shirts with red neckerchiefs, sort of the clean up crew. I don't know why they are called "monkeys," wise or otherwise.

That's just what they call them.

Monosabio duties include guiding the picador's horses to and from the bull, and hitching up the dead bull's horns to a rig attached to beribboned horses, then dragging the bull off with a snap of a whip.

They are accompanied by some plaza groundskeepers. These are the grunts who rake the sand to disperse the copious bull blood after the beast's been dispatched.

The procession done, everybody quickly exits, including the matador who's got the first bull and his *cuadrilla*, and they all retreat behind the wood *tablas* leaving the sands bare.

The *tablas* is a red painted wood wall about five feet high that circles the arena, fencing off the sandy fighting area.

At fifty-foot intervals this protective wall is broken up by *burladeros*, wood openings big enough to let a fleeing man through on either side but too small for a bull to pass through.

Think of them as escape hatches.

Behind this wall is the *callejón*, the alleyway where the matador and his guys rest between acts or escape to, if the bull is kicking some *torero* butt.

You and I are safely seated above the *callejón*, because the seating is protected by another wall about seven feet high that forms the back of the *callejón* alley.

Basically, there are two solid wood walls between us and the sands of arena to make sure we are safe and well protected from the bull.

In a moment, you will feel like two solid walls are not even close to enough. Maybe ten solid walls might do it

A high trumpet sounds a nine-note figure. My Spanish friends tell me the trumpet is singing "Ta-da-da-dee, *el toro va salir* or " Ta-da-da-de, the bull is coming out."

A red wood gate is swung open, all eyes turn to stare at the ominous darkness behind it.

And hooved Death itself comes charging out.

As you sit on the cold stone seat next to me, your eyes widen in fear, your heart starts to pound, adrenalin pumping overtime you break out in a cold sweat, and you get this tingling feeling in your groin like you might just pee in your pants.

You are frightened to the very brink of death.

And you hope to hell that those two flimsy walls will be enough to keep this evil thing from you.

Because a full blown, pissed off fighting bull is one of the most terrifying things you will ever see.

Ever.

It is two thousand pounds of pure sinewy black muscle, charging furiously this way and that, faster than a purebred race horse, looking wildly around, waving huge, ugly, sharp-pointed horns, snorting and glaringly looking for something, anything, to make even the slightest little movement.

So it can spear that thing with its sharp horns.

And toss it high into the air.

And gore it again when the thing falls. And again. And again.

Till it is a broken and bloody and smashed thing and is thoroughly dead.

Wherever in the arena you are, it just about scares the piss out of you every single moment of the bullfight. Because no way do you feel safe while that huge, blood-thirsty black monster out there rages for something to kill.

You will feel that way all fight long. Until this evil killing machine from hell is dead. Then for a moment you feel safe once again and can breathe.

Till the next bull enters.

Let's imagine this is the fifth time in this historic event you have felt that same scared, close-to-yellow-underpants, feeling in your groin.

You and I have watched the older Dominguin deal bravely with a difficult bull first up, then young Ordonez cuts an impressive two ears with his first, then Dominguin raises the bar with two ears and a tail from his second bull.

Unfazed, Ordonez ups the ante on the old pro with his next bull winning all Dominguín did, plus a rare hoof. Bull after bull each matador ratchets the contest up a notch, like some kind of insane poker game where the ante keeps going up with each card dealt and a bad hand will kill you.

Literally.

Now with the fifth, and his last, bull it's all up to Dominguín to reach down and come up with the very best goods he's got. And, unfortunately for him, you and I have just seen the baddest bull of all creation roar in with murder on its mind, looking every which way for something to gore to death, and hooking wildly in every direction.

Just when you're telling yourself that this particular beast is far too evil and huge to fight, that they'll have to pass on this raging monster and get another more reasonable one, Dominguín, motions to one of his *cuadrilla* to give the bull a look see.

The *matador* wants to learn which way it really hooks and how it does things before he tackles it himself.

The skinny member of his *cuadrilla* steps cautiously from out from behind the *burladero*, holding a huge yellow and vermillion cape called a *verónica* out in front of him for protection.

He yells at the bull, which at this point is looking desperately for something to kill on the other side of the ring.

At the sound of the *torero's* voice, the bull whips his head around to fix his evil eyes on him.

Something to gore to death?

Without hesitation, it charges across the arena, covering the ground in nothing flat, and lowers its sharp horns to skewer his hapless victim.

The *cuadrilla* member decides to pass him to his left, swinging the verónica that way.

Bad choice.

The bull hooks inside, tearing the cape and ripping it viciously from the startled man's hands. The bull spins around, spots the now defenseless man alone on the sand, and charges like a black fury from hell.

His eyes white with fear, the skinny guy sprints for his life to the wooden wall, never mind the *burladero*, and vaults over it inches from a deadly swipe of the bulls razor sharp horns, a swipe so fast you hear the wind swoosh.

Guess they know which way he hooks now. Every way.

It's insanity to go on with a bull like this one, there's no earthly way to fight it and live, not when you see what it did to the *matador's cuadrilla* member. He just barely escaped with his life.

That's when Dominguín himself steps from behind the *burladero*.

Is he mad? Has he lost his senses? Wait a minute, what's this?!

He gets on his knees in the sand, spreading the cape out before him, kneeling there, defenseless in front of the very angel of death. He yells for the bull's attention and you cringe.

Today you are going to see a man die. Right now, right here.

The bull spots him, wheels and charges with the fury of the devil. You wait for the razor sharp horns to sink into the poor guy's body, ripping it to shreds.

Desperately trying to save himself, the old pro makes a hopeless, last minute wave of the cape, but the huge snorting bull charges malevolently forward relentlessly targeting the billowing red and yellow cloth.

And misses him.

The crowd goes ape shit. This flesh and blood *torero* is a god of the ring.

The old man still has it. And how.

The deity springs to his feet and puts the enraged beast through a graceful series of passes, planting his feet firmly in the sand, each time the animal's horns clearing his body by scant inches. You and I hold our breath with each consecutive pass.

In today's fight you and I witness the classic *verónicas,* where the bullfighter holds the cape forward with two hands, as Veronica is said to have held out Jesus's burial shroud.

He shakes the large cape to *citar* the bull, or gain it's attention. This to us is the last thing on earth any sane person would do, the prudent thing would be to tiptoe silently away from the bull, hoping to escape its notice.

Then as the huge beast charges angrily to murder him, Dominguín calmly plants a foot to the side and swings the cape that direction leading the bull with it. It hooks wildly as it wooshes by, hoping to spear something.

We also see daring *chiquelinas*, invented by a matador called Chicuelo.

In this one, the torero starts a *verónica* and, as the bull charges at him, he quickly spins his body away from the bull, wrapping the cape tightly around him, making the cape for the moment seem to magically disappear, leaving only the *matador* standing there all alone on the sand wrapped in a cloth death shroud.

Somehow, and miraculously, when properly done the bull whizzes right by the cape-covered man. Then the torero twirls the other way, unfurling his cape and turns to face the whirling bull once again.

After a series of passes like these, with the last pass the matador swings the huge cape around and around in a whirling arc of yellow and vermillion cloth, in a breathtaking maneuver called a *rebolera*.

The bull stops in the sand, mesmerized and confused by the pinwheeling cape.

Arching his back and holding his head up to acknowledge the wild cheers of the crowd, the matador turns his back on the bull and stands there defenseless.

Is Dominguin mad ? Now the animal can gore him from behind.

Why it doesn't and how he knows it won't, *quien sabe*.

But we've just seen a guy with a lot of *cojones* do one of the most brilliant opening acts with a bull you could imagine. Ordonez already has his work cut out for him when he gets to his last bull.

And Dominguin has only started on his.

Me, by the time I see these gods of the ring, I've already been to enough big time bullfights to know more about this sport than I ever did about baseball or football. A bit of Spanish soul is beginning to pull me away from my all-American roots.

I've seen some of the masters of the taurine arts at work, guys like the South American part-Indian brothers César and Curro Girón, Spain's Antonio Bienvenida, Juan Belmonte and now, in this *mano a mano* of the decade, if not the century, the true bullfighting legends Antonio Ordonez and Luis Miguel Dominguín.

This bullfight series prompts America's "Life" magazine to engage Ernest Hemingway himself to cover the series of duels held between the two all around Spain this hot summer. From the *callejon* the famous writer watches and "Life" runs it as a three-part series (and later it's a book) called "The Dangerous Summer."

Here in Malaga at this bullfight you and I can see the great writer, "Papa" Hemingway, white beard and all and wearing a tan safari jacket, down there standing by the fence of the *callejon,* where they let the journalists view the action up close.

I see all this legendary bullfighting and I get into it with the unquestioning mind of a child, unencumbered by more American concepts of animal rights.

I reason that, if all these grownup people think it's a beautiful thing to kill an animal in this fashion, then it must be an okay thing.

After all, they're the grownups, they run this place. I'm just a kid.

And, unencumbered by any sort of animal rights kind of doubts; I am able to appreciate the artistry and the beauty that have captivated Spanish audiences for four hundred years.

Later, when I return from college as a grownup, more or less, my empathy for the animal will diminish my capacity to appreciate the raw and savage beauty of this spectacle. Cruelty kind of spoils the spectacle.

But that will be then. This is now.

So sit there in your cold stone seat next to me and let the *corrida* proceed.

Now, a trumpet sounds and the last part of the first act begins.

Two corpulent *picadors* ride their candidates for the glue factory through a gate into the ring, while the matador's *cuadrilla* keeps the bull busy on the other side. The two horses head in opposite directions around the perimeters of the ring.

Wearing blinders, lest they get a look at the dangerous bull and, quite understandably, freak out and bolt, the horses are heavily padded on their right side and front with cotton-padded canvas called a *"peto"*.

On this same side, the picador's leg is encased in tan-colored metal *"hierro"* or armor. His other leg has a smaller *"hierro"* to keep it from getting crushed when the bull slams the horse and rider hard against the *tablas.*

Sensing motion, the bull wheels around and spots the horse heading counter-clockwise around the ring. The poor nag is vulnerable, it's unpadded side facing the monster.

The snorting, horned beast charges towards the horse, closing quickly on the naked side of the unsuspecting nag, as the picador tugs frantically at the reins to turn the struggling, whinnying horse to its protected side, while the *monosabio* tries to shove it into place and then flee to safety.

The nag turns just before the bull hits.

The sharp horns slam into the padded side of the startled horse, picking it up off its feet and shoving it with a whack into the wooden *burladero.*

The surprised horse whinnies in fear and pain.

As the bull shoves and twists trying to sink a horn into the steed, and the horse desperately struggles to keep its feet, the *picador* leans over and spears the point of his lance down the bull's back, right where the shoulder muscles are.

The hefty man leans hard on the lance's wood shaft and a stream of blood begins to course down the bull's side.

This is the *picadors* job: to pierce and cut at the bull's shoulder muscles, weakening it to the point where the matador can deal with it and finish it off when the time comes.

The more the picador cuts, the less bull there is to fight. That's why, after a cut or two, the crowd will begin to whistle and shout disapprovingly, heaping their scorn on the fat guy with the lance.

Being a *picador* is not a very rewarding job and there's one other huge drawback: if the horse goes down, the *picador* can't easily run and jump over the fence with his right leg firmly encased in metal. The bull can make a meal of him.

Today that won't happen, as Dominguín waves the horsemen away after just a little picking. He wants a lot of bull left to work with and the crowd roars its approval.

The wounded, bleeding bull pants hard and looks angrily around to see what's next. He's got plenty of fight left.

Now the next part of the bullfight, *banderillas.*

These are twin two-foot long wooden sticks with barbed metal ends and colorful paper ribbons up and down the shafts. They are held, barb facing downward, by the top of the shaft, one in each hand, usually by a member of the matador's *cuadrilla*, sometimes as in the case of graceful showman Curro Girón, by the matador himself.

Here's the catch: holding a little spear in each hand, you can't also hold a cape. You stand nakedly on the hot arena sands to face the murderous bull without any apparent defense.

It looks like suicide.

The idea is to catch the bull's attention by shouting at him, *"Aah-hey, toro!!"* jumping up and down waving these long, colorful sticks.

When the raging beast angrily charges to kill you, and every instinct in your body screams at you to run away for your very life, you do exactly the opposite.

You run full tilt in the direction of his sharp deadly horns, heading slightly to one side, telling yourself over and over that a man can always turn tighter than a bull can.

As you run by, turning tightly inches from his ugly horns, you sink the sharp spear tips hard in his back and, as the enraged bull bucks in pain and surprise distracted by the burning barbs stinging him, you sprint away for your life towards the *tablas,* hoping he's not following.

That's called putting them in *al cuarteo*.

Another way to do it is called *al quiebro*.

In this one, you just stand there, maybe jumping up and down to get the bull's attention. When he naturally charges ferociously at you gathering speed alarmingly, you still just stand there like a dummy.

When he gets so close it looks like you're dead meat, you fake a move to one side, sticking out your foot and leaning that way.

Pray the bull buys it and veers that way, because you're going to spring back and stick the barbs in as he hurtles by. Then you run like hell because he's going to be in pain and really pissed off.

You can also plant the banderillas *dentro a fuera,* going in the small space between the bull and the wooden fence of the *tablas*, which cuts down your running room, if you are really daring or crazy, or maybe both.

Do this three times, all the while showing not a trace of fear and executing it with all the grace, style and poise of a ballet dancer.

Then, you are a *banderillero.*

Now it's time for the *faena*, the final act, the one in which the matador faces the bull all alone.

But first, he must dedicate the bull.

This part always looks a little too dangerous for my liking.

Sword and cape in his left hand, hat off held in his right hand, the matador offers his back to the bull and faces the audience where the person he wants to dedicate this bull and performance sits. It's a high honor for that person. It also looks dangerous for the torero to have his back to the bull.

Fortunately, Dominguín's *cuadrilla* keep the animal distracted as he recites a few words of dedication.

Then the matador throws his hat over his shoulder. If it lands right side up it means good luck, upside down is bad luck, *muy malo*.

It lands right side up. *Buena fortuna* for the old pro.

Next Dominguín exchanges the steel killing sword for a wooden bladed one, wooden so it weighs less while he works the bull until it's time for the kill and the steel blade, and he drapes over the wood sword a small red cape called a *capote.*

After the *veronica,* a big cape large enough to hide a couple of people behind, the *capote* looks impossibly small, nothing anyone in their right mind would hope could distract an enraged fighting bull.

As each matador makes this change to a tiny cape at this point in the fight, you want to stand up and tell them so. "Hey, guys! That's just crazy!"

Without hesitation, Dominguín strides over to the bull, which is standing, panting and bloody, near the wooden burladero. Luis Miguel has clearly lost his mind because he puts his back against the wall, leaving himself no room to retreat and yells loudly for the bull's attention.

This is madness.

His loud yell works and the bull charges right at him.

With a wave of the diminutive cape he leads it just past him, inches to go. By a miracle he survives, if the bull came a few inches further in, he wouldn't be able to back up out of its way. The wall is at his back, blocking any retreat.

Then Dominguin does something even crazier: he stays there, back against the wooden wall.

The bull has turned and studies that human thing that taunts him. He looks at the man. Then the cape. Then the man. Then the cape and the man again.

The panting bull seems to settle on the man and paws the sand with his hoof ready to charge. Just as he does,

Dominguín shakes the cape and the bull goes for the cape instead, inches from him.

He does the same insanely dangerous pass again. And again. For a total of five times.

With each pass the Málaga crowd goes crazier and crazier, erupting with ecstatic *"olés"*, each successively louder, building to a crescendo yell that must surely wake any buried Moors in the Gibralfaro castle high up above us on the hill.

Then after the fifth pass the bull stands there kind of puzzled and Dominguin steps out to the thunderous roar and applause of the crowd.

This man is genius.

Now, expertly using his cape, he works the bull to the center of the ring as the bullring band strikes up a stirringly heroic *pasodoble.*

The old bullfighting pro, still every inch the master, begins a series of classic passes of sheer poetry and magic. And the crowd and their *olés!* and the music and the man and the bull in the golden sun become one indescribably beautiful moment of pure Spanish soul.

That's when the bull gets him.

You and I see it in horror from our seats up above, Hemingway describes it from his much closer vantage point in the *callejón*:

"From where I was leaning on the fence the horn seemed to go into his body and the bull tossed him a good six feet or more into the air. His arms and legs were spread wide, the sword and muleta were thrown clear and he fell on his head."

The crowd screams in shock and fear, there is a flurry of capes and desperately running men and frantic shouts as Dominguin's cuadrilla try to pluck him from the clasp of death.

And Dominguin stands up, unbloodied.

The deadly horn miraculously went between his legs and missed him entirely.

Acting as if nothing happened, he waves everyone brusquely away, like 'What are you guys doing here!" and goes on with his *faena*.

You and I and the crowd catch our collective breath, hearts furiously pounding as if they would explode from our chests.

Graceful pass follows graceful pass, each punctuated by the roar of *"Ole!"*, building to a deafening crescendo when Dominguín completes a series of passes with one beautiful flourish and walks away in triumph, the bull just standing there confused for a moment.

Any number of times you see the bull glance from the offered cape to look hard at the man standing there, and you are sure he has figured out the game and will spear the *matador*.

Just as many times Dominguín convinces the beast instead to commit to yet another balletic series of passes. On several of these the bull brushes so close to the torero his suit of lights is stained red with its blood.

Now, the moment of truth.

This is the time when only a clean kill will validate everything Dominguín has achieved so far with this bull. In a true big time corrida, this is make-or-break, do-or-die, all the marbles.

If you can't make a clean kill, you got *nada.*

Exchanging his light, wooden sword for the real thing in a sharply honed steel that flashes blindlingly in the sun, Dominguín lines the panting bull up.

The animal's forefeet must be tight together as this will spread apart his shoulder blades, making a space for the sharp steel to sink in. Otherwise the blade will hit bone and spring out. Shaking his cape, the veteran moves the bull this way and that till it stands feet together.

With the rest of the crowd, you hold your breath.

Dominguin aims, or *punteas*, with the sword. He cocks his left knee, ready.

Gracefully, he swings the cape under the bull's nose and as it looks at the red cloth, Dominguin swiftly lunges dangerously over the animal's sharp right horn.

He sinks the sword in up to its red hilt.

The bull's eyes bulge wide and it staggers.

As members of Dominguín's *cuadrilla* wave capes at it, the bull makes weak feints to the right and left and then collapses to the ground, finished, at the matador's feet.

Dominguín arches his back and holds his hands up high to the heavens in triumph.

As a *torero* administers an almost unnecessary *coup de grace* with a dagger, and the bull stiffens and kicks its last, the crowd goes bananas, screaming and shouting their admiration, waving a sea of white handkerchiefs as a signal to *el presidente* to reward the valiant matador with some part of this very brave and noble bull.

Moments later, the bull's bloody severed ears, tail and a hoof in hand, Dominguín circles the arena with his *cuadrilla* to the madly roaring applause of the crowd.

They shower him with more than just cheers and wild clapping. Hats and flowers rain down, so do leather *botas* full of wine, even ladies undergarments.

In front of where we sit, Dominguin lifts one of the soft leather *botas* of wine and drinks a triumphant stream of *vino tinto*.

Then he throws one of the severed and still bleeding ears up high above us into the crowd to be caught by some lucky soul.

A splatter of the bull's blood hits my shirt.

"Olé!"

Believe it or not with his next bull, the last of the fight, Ordoñez turns in a performance of equal brilliance, minus the getting tossed by the bull part.

By the end of the *corrida*, these two legends of the ring will have cut an unheard of ten ears, four tails and two hooves.

Una maravilla!

The crowd is so hysterically joyous that the two bullfighters, and the chief herdsman of the *ganadería* that raised these magnificent bulls, are carried *en hombros* from the plaza, on the shoulders of the crowd, and paraded ecstatically through the streets of Málaga all the way to their hotel, celebratory throngs cheering wildly and applauding as they go.

While the bullfight press falls all over itself in colorful prose describing this historic event, I think one simple phrase from Hemingway (and isn't that what he wrote so brilliantly) sums it up quite succinctly:

"It was one of the greatest bullfights I have ever seen."

Now, in these pages, you've sat there and watched it with me and I hope you've enjoyed it.

For me it's not a bad tally for a scrawny ten-year-old from Chevy Chase, Maryland. I've seen Mickey Mantle at the plate in Griffiths Park in Washington, D.C.

And Dominguín and Ordoñez on the golden sands of the Plaza de Toros de Málaga.

One kid. Three gods.

Torremolinos

David M. Johnson

18
Los Desastres

TAKE THE TWO-LANE CARRETERA out of town east towards Málaga and, after four miles or so of farmer's fields, the airport is on your left behind a chain link fence. It's built around one medium-length runway that points, on one side to the sea and, on the other, inland towards the distant peaks of the Sierra Morenas.

On the Málaga side of this runway is the passenger terminal, little more than a white stucco building with a red brick tiled roof. You walk from this building across the tarmac to get to your plane. If you were expecting such things as automatic gangways and banks of television monitors showing departures and arrivals, you have to remember where and when this is.

On the other side of the runway is a Spanish Air Force base with a neatly lined up squadron of twin-engine Heinkel bombers, several of which played Nazi aircraft in the movie "Patton".

This is where my best friend Manolito's dad Juan heads whenever he checks in for duty. He goes to this Spanish military base.

Then he catches a military plane to his home base in Jerez, or if he's flown his three-engine Junkers in, he pilots that clattering contraption back. While Juan's away we have to suspend our adventures flying model airplanes and, if we have any new aeronautical or model-making questions, we wait impatiently for his return.

Because he's the pilot, he's the man who knows, the guy who's like a father to me.

To get to the base, he simply catches the local bus in the Plaza Central just past the El Mañana nightclub. It's a four or five mile ride down the coastal carretera to the base from the plaza.

This is where Juan is standing one day, waiting for the bus, when he collapses to the ground in the grip of a massive cerebral hemorrhage.

And dies on the spot.

Some village kids find me on the porch of our house behind the church and tell me the news straight away. In Torremolinos everybody seems to know who's who and what's going on.

Quién es quién y qué pasa.

So they know to tell me, Manolito's friend, the black news, and add that my friend and his mother are at the town doctor's office by the railroad tracks.

I stand outside the office with a crowd of people who have heard the news. Once, when the door opens to admit some local official I get a glimpse of Manolito's grief-stricken face inside. I try to signal some support but I don't know if he even sees me in the crowd.

Then Manolito and his mom Marula are gone from the village. The funeral is held in Jerez and I send a card and flowers. Manolito and his mom move away to be with relatives in La Linea, a colorless town that links Gibraltar to Spain.

I have, in one fell swoop, lost the company of my best friend Manolito and in his dad a father figure who filled in some of the gaps left by the absence of my own.

He is the one and only man in our Torremolinos world I looked up to and could trust in all our time there. In the ex-pat world there was no one who seems much of anything to me, just a bunch of shallow partiers, drunks, cheaters, liars, swindlers and bums.

Juan was a solid man.

Now the one real man I know, the one who somehow connected me with his love and support to my own father back in America, is gone.

And I am alone in this foreign land again.

Un desastre. A disaster.

You can't predict these things. Sometimes life just deals out a black card and that's the way it is. *Asi es.*

In Torremolinos the way it is also seems to include everyone being in on the bad news the instant it happens. Somehow, everybody just kind of knows, Spanish village telepathy.

Like the time on a late summer afternoon when crowds of us line the highway and look towards the west. We are waiting for the car with the victims of the latest *desastre* to come by. There's an air of dark excitement and blood and death, and we know all the details.

Two young couples from Málaga come down the coast to enjoy a day at the beach on their Sunday off. They go to one of the many cliff-lined beaches, like Torre Quebrada. And, since the day is hot, they set up their towels and stuff in the cool shaded sand under an overhang that has been there forever in the ancient rock cliff.

Forever ends that afternoon.

There is a loud crack and a rumble.

And both the young couples are crushed and buried beneath a piece of jagged, falling cliff weighing tons and tons.

Now rescue workers are digging frantically in the wet sand and working to get them out to see if any of the four have by some miracle survived.

Throngs of us are waiting in the *Plaza Central* for a car to rush by to the hospital in Málaga with whomever they pull out from under the slab of cliff. In Torremolinos there are no ambulances, just whatever car can be commandered on the scene.

And here it comes, racing up the highway, the driver beeping the horn repeatedly and desperately. Out the window he holds a white handkerchief, the local symbol that, along with the rapid honks, says this civilian car is, at this moment, an ambulance.

The car rushes by to Málaga and it isn't long before we learn that the first couple they extricated was in that vehicle. And that they both were DOA, *muertos.*

The fate of the other two will be similar. And, for all of us gathered along the highway in Torremolinos, their deaths are part of our lives.

We share in the tragedy. It is ours as well as the victims. We can practically breathe it.

And we talk with our friends about it's meaning. Why those four young people just staring out in life? What had they done to be dealt this card?

Why did they choose that beach and to be under that precise part of the cliff, instead of swimming, at that exact moment? Why did the rock wait thousands of years to fall on a Sunday when every other day of the week the beach is empty?

What is the meaning of this black event, this *desastre*?

If this was the hand of God, why did He reach down and crush these poor *Malagueños* to death in the sand?

It's a tragedy. *Un desastre* that gets an entire town caught up in its unfolding as the news breaks slowly, grim detail by detail.

Another time, the whole village is taken by surprise.

It's one more sunny day with the promise of warm, caressing breezes. Our mother is away for days on one of her many extended trips with her ex-pat party gang, leaving the maid in charge at home.

Suddenly the gentle sea breezes are blown away by a cold, hard wind that creeps in from the sea.

Out in the Mediterranean, masses of angry dark clouds approach, whirling with evil intent and lit by flash after flash of white-hot lightning. In moments, the day turns as dark as any cold moonlit night.

You run for home and shut the door just as the storm breaks with a howling fury of its wind and the massive crash of thunderclaps one after another.

First, driving rain pelts and floods the town, making rivers in the streets, then hail hammers at the windows, actually cracking some and breaking one upstairs.

The bone white flashes of lightning are followed without hesitation by exploding thunderbolts so close they send shivers deep inside you, shaking the windows, as you huddle with your brother and sister and the maid.

The storm goes around and around the town, as if hunting for victims and bones to break and blood to drink. You just pray that it will go away.

When the maelstrom finally does recede, with farewell parting rumbles of thunder, you venture out to find a world transformed.

Red rivers course through the streets. Here and there, they have brought streams of red mud down the hills to choke the roads and pull down walls and houses.

When you look out over the beach from the tower lookout, the calm, friendly Mediterranean is gone.

In its place is a maelstrom, boiling with huge white angry waves that wash over the entire beach. A quarter mile up the sands towards Malaga, a fifty-foot white, two-masted schooner lies on its side, driven ashore in the storm and washed all the way up to the road, beached like a huge white whale.

The reports begin to come in.

Up in the hills, lightning bolts killed several mules in the fields, just about fried them. On the road to Fuengirola, two buildings are on fire. Flooding is everywhere, with some areas swamped with thick, red mud.

Three fishing boats are missing, presumed sunk. The angry seas hurtled into the low-lying streets of the Carihuela fishing village.

In one fisherman's simple one room house, a massive rogue wave broke down the door, grabbed a screaming toddler and, before his mother could reach him, swept him out to sea. The little child is never seen again.

La vida es dura. Life is hard.

This is a lesson that *los desastres*, big and small, public and not-so public, bring home to you in Torremolinos. There are a more than a few images that become engraved in my mind:

- A mule driver, wearing his woven hemp and cloth sandals, whacks his lead animal, part of an in-line train of four mules that strain to pull a heavy cart of red bricks up the hill by the church.

Running up the road to urge on another of the reluctant beasts, the man's cheap sandals slip on the sandy cement road and he falls.

As Mark and I watch from the steps of our home in horror, the mules pull the heavily laden cart of bricks over the fallen mule driver and the big wooden wheel with it's outer layer of hard steel plate crunches over his back. He lies motionless in the street as his assistant boy screams for help.

- Manolito and I are by the cemetery, where the dull light yellow dirt road leads down to the beach. We hear a man yelling and a woman scream and we hide by some trees.

The town drunk comes down the road, hauling his crying barefoot wife roughly by the arm. She is sobbing and afraid. Her white shirt is torn and her dress is smeared with dirt.

In his other hand, the *borracho* holds a wide brown leather belt , thick and tough looking.

As we watch, he hits her on the face with it, hard and she cries out.

"Whack!"

She falls down in the dirt and he whacks her again. She cries out and raises her dust-covered arm to ward off the blow, sobbing for mercy. He raises the belt again and lands another, even more vicious blow.

She raises her arm again, begging for mercy. She gets none.

And my mind's camera snaps an image I will never forget, a picture that says nobody should ever be able to treat a pleading, sobbing human being, especially a woman, like this.

But nonetheless, there it is.

Another time the disaster is invisible despite being in plain sight.

- Some young Spanish friends and I, we supply ourselves with a bottle of Málaga Dulce sherry from the Bar Quitapenas. At this time and place, children can buy alcohol anywhere without question. They probably assume it's for Dad or just don't care.

Thus provisioned for our trek, about 30 of us bike out of Torremolinos proper and head west down the long hill past the Carihuela fishing village and along a stretch of highway with small vacation villas either side belonging to rich Spaniards from Madrid and elsewhere.

After about a kilometer we stop to share a pull on the bottle of sweet sherry, the alcohol burning the back of our young throats. As we look towards the seashore we are amazed to see something that is totally out of place to us in 1959 Torremolinos.

Rising above the one-story villas and small *casitas* is the white skeleton of a building going up like nothing else anywhere on the *Costa*: in a land of one and two story buildings it is a whopping 10 stories high.

One of my Spanish friends says it's to be a hotel called the *Hotel Pez Espada*, or Swordfish Hotel.

None of us knows at the time, but this skeleton is a harbinger of the death of the small world that surrounds it, for it will swiftly be followed by hordes of other gargantuan tourist hotels that will swallow this simple village whole and spit it out on the altar of cheap mass tourism.

The village that we arrived at in 1957 will be near unrecognizable by the mid 1960s and almost totally so as the 1970's progress.

Standing there with my bike and my local friends, I am unaware that the village I'm beginning to feel part of will soon be as gone as my one-time American Davey Crockett life.

Shape of things to come. Pez Espada, first multi story hotel.

Why am I taking you here?

Because I want to show you all of Torremolinos and not spare you the parts that aren't graceful and pretty.

And that includes *los desastres*

Like I said, in Torremolinos, they are usually public knowledge. But some, like the drunk with the belt, are more hidden and private.

This is one of those.

One evening, fresh from playing with friends in the square near the church, I head home, maybe ten o'clock at night, nobody much pays attention to how late I come home, at 10 years of age I can pretty make my own hours and go where I please. I traipse down the stone steps that descend the cliff to the left of the church.

Halfway down, descending into the dark of the evening, I go through the gate marked *"Huerta Alta"* that marks the gardens of our cliffside house.

I tread down the steel steps that descend to the garden and crunch across the pebbled path that leads to our three story white-washed adobe villa.

Up ahead, there are warm, yellow lights on, my mother will probably be back. She and some ex-pat friends went away for the afternoon to Málaga to tour some local vineyards and wineries.

But now after a day of adventure she's returned.

As I draw near the house, one of her English friends, we'll call him Jess Farris, his wife Julie nowhere in sight, weaves down the path. Catching sight of me, he smiles and wobbles.

"Ah, David. Come over here. I need to talk to you about something."

I'm not sure about this. He looks odd, he's not standing straight. But he's a grownup and he needs to talk to me. Maybe something bad has happened to my mother. My heart sinks.

"Come over here. This is important. I have to tell you something. Sit down here."

He leads me to a dark corner of the garden, under the cliffs and makes me sit down on a small stone bench.

"There is something important I need to tell you."

Shit. I knew it.

There's been an accident, my mother has been hurt. Or even worse. I look up to him to accept the bad news. I'm a man I can take it.

He grabs my head roughly with one hand, my right wrist with the other and pulls me to him.

He kisses me hard and I feel something large and slimy ooze down my throat, choking me. It's his tongue. I gag at the taste of old wine and stale spit.

He pulls back for a second, then grabs my head again, repeating the kiss as he presses my little hand in between his legs to feel something hard there.

He kisses me again and again as I nearly throw up.

For a few drunken seconds, he comes up for air, and I am half retching from the taste in my mouth as he drunkenly glances back at the house and slurs to me:

"Do you....do you think the family are watching?"

His hands have for a brief second loosened on me and without a word I bolt for the house, my feet pounding on the loose gravel, my heart pounding with the fear he will follow.

Believe it or not, that's not the worst part.

When I get to the house I find Mark and Mimi already there. I stammer some words about what just happened. They say something about Mom being really drunk, not being herself, but she's upstairs. We run up the stairs to tell her what has happened, to look for protection.

She is upstairs lying on a couch, barely conscious.

Apparently their tour of the vineyards has included enough samplings of potent Malaga wine to kill an elephant. My mother, like her friends, is roaring drunk.

I don't know this. I had never before seen my mother this drunk. She does drink and get funny and tipsy, but she doesn't usually get drunk like this, that's not her style. This is something as rare as when that piece of jagged cliff snapped and fell on the bathers from Malaga.

We try to get her attention and tell her what Jess Ferris has done to me.

She turns her head slowly and her eyes blink rapidly. She doesn't understand a word we are saying. She stammers something incoherent about the winery.

I realize that talking to her now is pointless.

I go to my bed and cower in fear under the sheets through a long sleepless night.

The next morning my mother is recovering over a coffee in the kitchen.

I go to her and tell her what Jess did to me in the night, how he dragged me into the darkness and shoved his wine-soaked tongue down my ten-year-old throat and shoved my hand in his crotch.

I want her to make sense of this. To tell me I'll be okay. That it doesn't mean something bad about me, that I won't have to be gay now, that I haven't been somehow infected with this horrid man's disease.

She looks at me without saying anything for a few moments, then looks away, her face expressionless, and sips her coffee.

She examines her fingernails for a terribly long time.

Then she puts down her coffee and motions for me to follow her into the basement stairway that leads down from the kitchen. She closes the basement door behind us.

I follow her down, past the shelves of canned food and rice, and pasta, the cooking implements, pots and pans.

When we get to the bottom she turns around and hits me hard across the face, so hard my cheek stings and I nearly fall down.

"Don't tell lies, you little fibber!" she yells at me.

She insists that this never happened and I should not ever again talk about something that isn't true, because that makes me a liar and that's a horrible thing to be.

When I start to say that it did happen, she hits me again repeatedly as I try to cover my face, backing away, knocking cans off the shelves.

She stares at me with eyes full of fury, shaking with rage.

"You will never, ever speak of this again! Not to your friends, or your brother and sister and never, _ever_ to me!" she commands me.

"It did not happen! It's a lie!"

"You will forget about any such thing. You will wipe it from your mind and never, ever say anything more about something that _did_..._not_..._happen_!"

"Do.....you....understand!"

I rub my face and run up the stairs and away, out into the garden and the bright sunlight, trying to process this dark thing I am supposed to do: to erase a horrid memory that's burning deep in my brain.

But I realize that's what I must do. I set my mind to it.

I am a good son. I do what my mother says, I try to forget about this shameful thing that has happened to me, maybe it was all my fault anyway, something stupid that I brought on myself.

I never talk about it to anyone for well into my adult life. It takes me time, and many weeks of worrying that this means something about me, that I am marked.

For months, I am tortured by a succession of crushing migraine headaches that send me fleeing to bed and darkened rooms, as I try to make my mind erase what happened and my wild fears about it.

Deep down inside it goes, my worry that somehow this guy, maybe his homosexual saliva, has infected me with some kind of gay germ or something.

I don't know what makes somebody gay and now I can't talk to anyone about this. Ever.

I am alone in a bleak wilderness, far from America with no friends, no one to run to. There is no USA or dad coming to save me, no hardy frontiersman who will protect me from the evil beasts that prowl this wild and dangerous place, nobody running up to protect me with his trusty musket in hand.

Davy Crocket is dead.

I do my best to bury this memory like you would the body of a cold dead child.

And, in a Catholic Spain, where even the *extranjeros* seem to laugh behind their hands whenever they talk about queers, I gather queerdom is a fate worse than death.

Better to be buried under a ton of rock from a cliff than to be gay. So I do what my mother says and work to bury the memory, banning it from my consciousness, telling myself to forget it as best I can.

Keep repeating it and it will be true: it never happened, it never happened, it never happened, it's a lie, it's a lie…. it…is.. a lie!

I forget, as best as I can. With some effort I succeed in blotting the memory out as I've been told to. For nearly thirty years. It never occurred. It never happened.

But it dogs my mind, prowling around in the dark regions of my being, making me stiffen in fear whenever the conversation turns to gays, but not knowing why it frightens me with sheer panic: will the gay saliva germ kick in now?! Will I become this horrible thing?!!!

In many ways, it ruins my young love life, makes me doubt myself and my masculinity.

It also makes it difficult for years to accept any gay people I meet without fear, to come to know them as friends and just people, not some horrible child attacking bogeymen.

Un desastre.

At the age of 35, well past most of that awful buried memory, happily married with kids, for no apparent reason, this memory will suddenly surface.

I feel kind of like someone who has been swimming underwater holding his breath in the murky depths for a long time and finally breaks the surface and gasps desperately for fresh air are after an eternity of not breathing.

And I will deal with it and do my best to work it out.

I learned as a young man that Jess Ferris is dead after having come out and left his gullible wife, Julie. He is found floating in a swimming pool by his gay houseboy. I don't rejoice in his death now but it seems like a pale glimmer of justice.

Hopefully he was not a regular abuser of young boys, but if he was he got what he deserved in the end.

My mother says nothing about it. Almost ever.

Back then, she probably chooses to ignore it as an inconvenient event that, if openly talked about, might ruin her social standing with the wonderful, Torremolinos party crowd, in which this closeted Englishman is a central figure.

Perhaps she talked to Jess about it, maybe that's why he never touched me again. Or, knowing her, perhaps not. It might have been socially awkward to bring it up.

Who knows.

She won't even apologize when I bring it up 25 years later, saying that I must be talking about someone else, not her good friend Jess who wouldn't do such a thing, and then switches the conversation to other topics as if nothing important happened.

I guess as far as she was concerned, nothing did.

For the adults involved, that's pretty much it.

That evening back then in Torremolinos, like my mother, Jess gets bushwhacked by one too many glasses of Málaga Dulce, and then wakes up the morning after and shakes off the memory like a nasty hangover.

Alcohol is a good excuse. For my mother, too. Drunk shit happens. Wake up and move on.

They didn't know what hit them. And neither did I.

We were three people who got swept up in an accident, nailed like those unlucky *Malagueño* beachgoers who were killed by a jagged piece of falling cliff.

Unfortunately, I'm the one who got crushed to death.

Asi es la vida.

Torremolinos

19
La Revuelta

I'M SITTING ON A COLD GREEN PLASTIC CHAIR in the middle of the Calle San Miguel right where it widens out near the old watchtower.

The old church looks the same as ever, and a soft Mediterranean early evening breeze drifts by smelling slightly salty just like it did when my friends and I played tag here, keeping a watchful eye out for cars.

I don't have to do that today. There will be no cars ever again.

Calle San Miguel, the bustling main street through Torremolinos, has become a pedestrian mall, full of strolling and shopping sun-burned tourists.

I'm sitting at an outdoor cafe outside of the white washed house where the two little old ladies in black used to sell candy and cigarettes, calling us kids *"angelitos"*.

Now there are no private houses on this stretch of Calle San Miguel, or anywhere for that matter, just one garish, neon, tarted up store after another selling cheap tourist trinkets, handmade candles, t-shirts, postcards, broken up by the many restaurants and bars with menus prominently promising "autentic Spanish paella" in German, French, Swedish and mis-spelled English. The sea air is mixed with the waxy scent of candles being handmade at one of the many nearby stalls selling junky tourist trinkets.

I haven't been here for nearly forty years.

This is my *revuelta* or return. That word in Spanish can also refer to things being scrambled, like eggs for instance.

And, *hombre*, both old Torremolinos and my distant memory of it have now been given a really thorough brain-scramblng *revuelta*. My mind is spinning madly.

My wife, Jill, and daughters, Rebecca and Emma, are here today in Torremolinos with me. They've come to see where Dad grew up in the late 1950's and early 60s.

I try to find things from back then to show them. It's not easy. My oldest daughter, Rebecca, sums it up with the honesty of a fifteen year old. "It's nothing like I imagined from your stories. I was sort of expecting to see a little village."

Here and there, where a crumbled piece of the past remains, I point out to my family where the village was, and they can make out the dim outline.

But time, and tourism, have nearly completely erased that simple place.

We have been on the Costa Del Sol nearly a week. After four cold and cloudy-grey days visiting Jill's family in England, we flew in to arrive at the Málaga airport at night.

It's now like any airport anywhere in the world, with all the requisite mod cons like automated jet ways, stainless steel baggage conveyors and banks of televised flight information.

The old whitewashed red-tiled building is long since

gone, as is the military base across the runway with the Nazi era planes.

Years ago they lengthened the runways to accommodate the largest of jets carrying hordes of sun-seeking tourists. One of the first planes to arrive actually landed by mistake in some of the newly poured concrete and made one of the shortest landings ever recorded.

We get a rental car and drive past Torremolinos into the night towards Marbella, where we have reservations at a luxury hotel called Puente Romana, that has the remains of an old Roman bridge.

I figure that along the highway, particularly as we pass through today's Torremolinos, I will probably recognize some landmarks, like the Plaza Central, the water fountain by the Banco de Vizcaya, or the dirt field where I used to fly model airplanes.

But nothing is familiar to me, maybe we have taken some by-pass, and we drive on through some light rain. In our ten days here, it's about the only precipitation we see.

The rest will be gloriously warm sunny days that stand in marked contrast to the damp grey gloom we left in England a short flight away.

It's easy to see why now there are over 400,000 English people, retired and otherwise, living in the Costa Del Sol. That's more than the cities of Liverpool and Birmingham combined.

You wonder if there's any room for the Spaniards, and we haven't even factored in the German's, Danes, Swedes and other Euros.

There are a lot of warmth-seeking people from chillier, darker countries here, drawn to the hot sun like so many cold coins to a Spanish magnet.

I have avoided actually coming to Torremolinos itself for four or five days. Maybe it wasn't that important.

Or perhaps it actually was.

Either way, we have pottered about Marbella, been up the twisty mountain road to Ronda and down the coast to Gibraltar.

I've gotten up in the morning and walked down to the Marbella beach to hear the gentle Mediterranean waves sing a song I knew so well many years ago.

I've tasted Andalusian cooking again, tried some of the *marisco's*, and had a cold beer *caña* or two at a bar. I think I've got my Southern Spain sea legs. So I propose that, one late afternoon, we pay Torremolinos itself a visit.

We drive up the coast and the highway is new and unfamiliar. I sort of get lost making my approach into an unfamiliar Torremolinos full of 20 story buildings and traffic lights and we drive down from the hill side.

We are probably coming in from the direction of what used to be the simple hill village, the *Calvario*, where that single dusty road led up past two rows of plain white-washed houses and the boys reformatory building.

It's hard to say, we are just driving past block after block of mega-story apartment buildings. I am flying blind, I turn the car by instinct.

This way, that way.

We reach a parking garage right by an X-rated video shop and I give up trying to find my way and turn in with a word to my family.

"Let's just walk from here. I think we're somewhere near the center of town."

We take a ticket from the automatic dispenser, leave the car, and proceed to walk on by foot. We pass a pharmacy, some restaurants and another shop with a sign marked "XXX" selling pornographic materials.

God, I think about the priest who cut the kisses between unmarried couples out of the movies, and banned that French bikini babe from the beach, what would he have to say about videos with couples actual doing it, and forget about the wedding rings, *padre*.

Cock rings more likely.

Two blocks on, we come to a sort of a square and something about it makes me pause.

Something in me says "Wait as minute."

Those tall trees in the island in the middle. That turn in the road over there. It's unmistakable. This is the Plaza Central, the very center of the village of Torremolinos, the square that dilapidated bus brought my family to way back in 1957.

Somehow, by blind instinct, I have got us to the old heart of the town of Torremolinos.

I look to the other side of the *carretera*, trying to find the Bar Central, the social hub of the town, the local watering hole, the ground zero of life itself, the place as kids we bitched about because it didn't offer hamburgers.

It's a McDonalds.

I have this brief flash of me as Charlton Hesston in a loincloth in "The Planet of The Apes", falling to my knees in the sand in front of the remains of the old Torremolinos watchtower, and shouting out

"My god, you fools! You fools!"

I have another flash of me and my brother and sister sipping *café con leches* at the Bar Central in 1958 and whining like little spoiled American brats about the menu.

"Geez. They don't even have any hamburgers."

They do now. And *Señor* Ronaldo McDonald included in the bargain.

I swallow my feelings and we walk on to the Calle San Miguel. It's like a neon pedestrian tunnel, full of trinket shops and slot machine parlors and cheap restaurants.

As my wife and kids stroll down it, I leave them to shoot a few pictures of the Plaza Central. I notice a bar across the street that's unchanged; it looks like it did that day we arrived across the street on the bus from Algeciras.

Years ago, my sister took flamenco lessons in a room upstairs. I go in and ask the barman what happened to the Bar Central. He tells me it moved elsewhere in town to another plaza

"Ya hace años." Years ago.

I notice that across the street the *marisquería* where I enjoyed fresh clams is still there. But next to it, a Wendy's. Not absolutely everything is gone, but pretty much. I hurry down San Miguel to catch up with Jill and the kids.

They are at the railroad crossing, or where it used to be.

There are no rails anymore, that magically puffing steam engine is long since gone, as is the modern diesel that killed the old man who mined the train tracks for bits of coal. Now it's just a street full of more shops with of more shiny stuff for tourists. The train runs underground and out of sight.

As we stroll down the street amid the throngs of visitors from Germany and Denmark and god knows where, I can call to mind what used to be there while I note what actually is:

The old bakery where the donkeys used to arrive with fragrant rosemary bushes from the mountains. A cute gift shop with ashtrays reading "I Came to the Costa Del Sol."

The Bar *Quitapenas*, where that long ago tourist parked his car on top of Titi's "motorcycle." A psychedelic poster shop.

Crazy Man's house, from where he used to lunge out at you in his retarded rage.

A jewelry shop advertising, "Joya cultured pearls" at "discount prices!!!"

The lumberyard, where I used to hear the whine of whirling blades rending wood while I took long drinks from the mountain spring-fed fountain. An *auténtico* Spanish restaurant featuring "reel Spanish dishes."

We continue our tour and I point out a few faded memories to my wife and kids.

Opposite the church, the houses are actually still the same. I can point out the balconies Mark and I clambered over like mischievous little monkeys after we set up Mimi to kill all her dolls.

And the church is just like it was.

Only, that's deceptive.

As the tourism money rolled into Torremolinos, the priest had the old church demolished and built a huge modern-looking big church in its place. The new one was so singularly hideous, and the public outcry so great, he was actually forced to tear it down and build a replica of the old church in its place.

Too bad they couldn't look at the whole town with the same critical eye.

Behind the church, our house that had the screening room for Mark's movies and the "science laboratory" is still kind of there.

Only, it has been gutted for reconstruction and the front door glass has Mastercard and American Express decals on it, indicating it has been used as a shop or restaurant.

Across the way, the house's private garden overlooking the sea, where Pacquito kissed Mimi and she got in trouble for it, is a two-story Chinese restaurant.

To it's right, the lookout by the old mill tower, Torremolino's namesake, is likewise taken over by a restaurant lit in bright neon.

From the railing at the top of the cliff, you used to be able to look across farm fields all the way to Málaga, with the majestic snow-covered Sierras Nevada mountains in the distance.

Now all you see is 20 and 30 story apartment buildings and hotels.

We descend the steps to the *Bahondillo* below. At the mid point I look to where we had a Cliffside house with a huge garden, *Huerta Alta*. The cliff itself is obscured by a huge hotel with many balconies. And where the gardens and house were now there are small apartment buildings.

At the bottom of the garden, there used to be a gypsy cave that people actually lived in. They must have blasted it away as now there's yet another building on its site.

We walk on down into the *Bahondillo* fishing village.

Just like Calle San Miguel, every single doorway where people used to live and sit out on the steps has become a store. Every inch of the fishing town I knew has been dedicated to trawling instead for tourist's pesetas.

Back up the cliff I find the graveyard still where it was, but without the massive iron gate, and surrounded by unremarkable modern buildings.

I doubt it's desolate enough to scare anyone now.

On our way out of town, I briefly head the car east towards Málaga, hoping to find the field Manolito and I first flew model planes in and where the rag tag circus pitched its tent every year.

All that's there now are more buildings I can't even recognize.

As we turn a corner near where the field must have been, we pass a heavily made-up streetwalker tottering on red high heel pumps.

Jill and I agree it is probably a man, and not a pretty one.

I hit the gas and we accelerate fast out of Torremolinos.

There had been here and there just enough scraps of the past that I could recall a little bit of the town I knew and loved. And conjure up a few memories.

But basically, the "simple town" Rebecca and Emma and Jill knew from my stories has been eradicated, steamrollered by modernity and time and tourism into junky gift shops and restaurants and cheap tacky neon nonsense.

It was bound to happen.

Back when my mother brought us here to begin with, we might have known Torremolinos was doomed by the fact that foreigners like us were there in the first place.

Who were we kidding.

We were like some foreign micro-organism invading a healthy person, germs that were about to quickly multiply and kill their unsuspecting host, the tip of a giant wave of tourism that was about to smack down ferociously on Torremolinos and drown its simple soul.

It had been discovered. And that was its undoing.

Makes me wonder if that mean kid back in 1957, the bully who punched me and Mark for being *"Americanos"* had some inkling or premonition of the awful threat we represented to his town. If I could travel back in time myself, I'd probably punch us both in the face, too, real hard.

But all the fists in the world wouldn't have staved off the inevitable.

Torremolinos had the bad luck of being a charming, sunny place that got written about and "discovered" just as the age of the jumbo charter jet dawned, and as people in Europe to the North began to have enough money to take vacations in sunny *España.*

That was the sad end of what to me was so pretty.

But they say beauty is in the eye of the beholder.

I'm sure if you're some poor working stiff in Germany or Britain and you're tired of the cold and the damp and the grey skies and your asshole of a boss, Torremolinos is probably a paradise today.

You and your buds can get some cash together, jet down to the beach, get horribly sunburned, then, to dull the pain from lobster-red skin, get shit-faced on cheap Spanish beer and chase skirts till you catch one or till you puke and/or pass out.

Then wake up the next sunny day and start all over again until your package tour runs out and it's back to the factory and the cold and the asshole of a boss.

For stuff like that who cares that the place looks like some tinny amusement park that bears very little resemblance to anything Spanish at all.

You don't give a big whoopee about actually being in Spain anyway. It could be anywhere sunny and cheap. You just want some sun and some fun and to maybe get laid.

It works out.

It's probably also a good deal for a lot of Spaniards.

When I was there, most local people were dirt poor and didn't have much prospect of earning money. The average Spanish annual income in 1958 was something like $200, and in Málaga probably even less.

Now tourism has helped lift Spain into the modern world, even into the European Common Market. The average annual income shot to $13,000 by the start of this century.

Every year there's well more than one tourist, closer to two, for every single one of the nearly forty million Spaniards, including 10 million Germans, nine million Brits and over 20 million French visitors.

To make sure these visitors have a good time, one out of every ten Spaniards works in the tourism industry.

So now, in Torremolinos like elsewhere, the local people have some real money. They can run gift shops or work in restaurants or find some other way of parting the rich *turistas* from their cash.

Then they can now buy things they couldn't before like maybe cars and TVs and iPhones and the like. Nobody wants to be poor. So I guess it's okay, even for Torremolinos.

To me ugly, *muy feo*, but okay for others.

Spain has also changed in so many other ways since we first arrived. Some of them beautiful indeed.

You won't find any portraits of Generalisimo Francisco Franco hanging around these days; they're gone, along with his statues. He died in 1975 and two days later Juan Carlos I became king of what in 1978 was declared a parliamentary democracy.

With some bumps and rough spots Spain has made it's way from a fascist dictatorship to a true democratic country.

And that's worked out pretty well, though my Spanish friends I keep in touch with routinely complain about the government.

There is a new freedom in politics, in the arts, in life in general.

The press can say anything it likes and there are no more censors in the post office ripping offending pages out of magazines. You can see a lot more than just kisses in the movies.

Spain also eventually shed that territory in the Spanish Sahara that I watched it's Hitler era bombers fly off to defend back in the 1950's.

In 1970 the Sawahari people living there organized massive demonstrations for freedom, which Spain put down in very bloody fashion. The Sawahari's didn't give up and six years later, worn down by intensifying guerrilla attacks, Spain threw in the towel and the last Spanish soldier left on Feb. 27, 1976.

This wasn't, however, the big happy ending for the Sawaharis.

Their neighbor to the North, Morocco, muscled right in and, from the south, Mauritania took a chunk.

Attracted in part by the Western Sahara's rich mineral deposits and well-stocked fishing grounds, Morocco sent masses of its people marching south in what they proudly call The Green March to "liberate" territory the Spanish had apparently just abandoned and that historically, so they said, actually belonged to Morocco.

That must have been a cold shock to the Sawaharis who've lived there for six centuries, fighting for their freedom and autonomy from Spain and now Morocco.

Today the Sawaharis fight a continuing guerilla war to gain control of a nation most of Africa and the United Nations agree is rightfully theirs by heritage, and neither Spain's nor Morocco's.

And the Sawahari women and children have lived for generations in wretched refugee camps in the hottest most inhospitable parts of the Sahara desert, on occasion fleeing from the Moroccan planes that roar in to bomb and strafe them.

When you think about that, you've got to agree there are much uglier fates in this world than just the tarted up touristization of Torremolinos.

And there are exiles far worse than a scrawny American kid in a Davy Crockett hat suddenly finding himself marooned in a little seaside Spanish village.

Hey, at least it wasn't the blazing Sahara and nobody bombed us.

And what about us, the Johnson's, did our decade in exile in Torremolinos, and later in Madrid, work out for us?

Well, we survived, that's something. We even did pretty well. Whether that's because of, or in spite of, our years living as essentially countryless nomads is up to debate.

Having lived as a rootless third culture kid I come down heavily on the "in spite of" camp. I know that because of my unusual upbringing I had to struggle with a pile of burdens for many years.

Can't say I saw enough positives to make it worthwhile. The one that comes the closest is the chance we had to get to know a sweet little village called Torremolinos. It was in many ways a magical place, one that I will always hold in my heart, even though being there wasn't necessarily good for us in other ways and later in life.

Some people say what doesn't kill you makes you stronger. I say, no, it just doesn't kill you, that's all. If anything, the ordeal makes you weaker, but you pick yourself up half dead, lick your wounds and get back in the fight, maybe limping a bit or missing an eye.

It does not make you stronger in my book. And Lord knows I have been there.

There's a pretty good, though dry and academic, book called "Third Culture Kids" about children who grew up like us: not in their own culture and really not in that of the foreign country they find themselves in, but in a curious in between ex-pat bubble, or a "Third Culture".

The book does a decent job of documenting the possible benefits as well as the many trials and emotional and social problems that come with the Third Culture kid territory.

Children, particularly adolescents, who yearn to belong, to feel part of a social context, who want to fit in, can come out emotionally scarred from the experience and the dislocation.

Our California friend, Laurie (Riddell) Geary from back in Torremolinos days says she does not look on the experience, particularly her time in a convent school, as very positive.

"Even though I have to admit Torremolinos itself was beautiful."

"The trauma of separating from my high school friends, the culture shock and isolation I felt at a time when social life was the most important thing in my life, were not worth the 'adventure'....."

Having raised her own sons in one place and in America she concludes: "There is nothing more rewarding than the stability of one's friendships and the chance to test one's abilities – intellectually, physically and socially......adolescents need that experience to best define their identities and build their self esteem."

"I'm sorry I missed that experience."

The book "The Third Culture Kids", with lots of research to back it up, cites feelings in people growing up like we did as ranging from adult depression and anger to inability to form relationships and feelings of grief, even mourning , for the lives they have lost, for the people they might have instead become.

Reading that book, I realized I have suffered from some of those feelings and have struggled hard to overcome them.

The three of us Johnsons shared at least some of that, right alongside the very unique childhood magic memories of a special place that Torremolinos was.

El Miko, my brother Mark has gone on to be a major success in Hollywood as a film and TV producer.

He says when he first and finally came back to America he had built it up so high in his imagination, creating a fabulous day dream country from all those Hollywood movies he saw about it, that he was very let down and disappointed by the humdrum reality and the lack of any real magic.

The highways cluttered with neon signs and strip malls, the uninspired houses in colorless suburban tracts, our father's redneck and racist neighbor who, though a dentist, insisted we address him as "Doctor" Chandler, this was not the dreamland he had expected.

"It all seemed pretty cheesy," he says.

Despite the original let down, Mark has gone on to scale the heights of Hollywood as a highly successful producer.

He won an Oscar for "Rain Man" and has done, among his many credits, "Donnie Brasco", "The Natural", "Good Morning Vietnam", "The Rookie", "The Notebook" and the Christmas 2005 mega blockbuster "Narnia: The Lion, The Witch and the Wardrobe."

Recently he won several Emmy's as executive producer of the international massive hit TV series "Breaking Bad."

Mark claims he's positive about our years in Spain, and asserts he wouldn't trade them for anything. He says he remembers a fun, sort of upbringing with our mother as a kookie "Auntie Mame" character.

Makes a nice Hollywood story.

However, Mark seems to have erased many of the details of this "fun life" from his memory, like some bad dream you try to forget.

Today he can't actually remember many details from Torremolinos or from our years abroad. I know. I quizzed him as I wrote this book, asking about specific things relating to him, events that I remember with absolute clarity yet he says he has no memory of them.

Several years ago, I came back from a high school reunion in Spain and told Mark about meeting the guy who was his best buddy back then. I gave his ex-classmate and pal Mark's phone number.

Some time later, my brother told me the old high school friend had called him. Mark said he vaguely remembered his name and he asked me who exactly he was. He said the guy kept describing experiences Mark just couldn't remember.

If life was so wonderful there, why has *El Miko* erased their memory?

Despite that fact Mark is absolutely certain he would not exchange our experiences in *España* for anything else.

He feels it has even served him well in many ways. One of those is that for the past 15 years, he has been Chair of the Foreign Language Film Selection Committee of the Motion Picture Academy. Mark says his international upbringing has been very helpful to him in that position.

My older brother does remember he felt very lonely and abandoned and angry over there. He says his way of dealing with growing up without our father and so much else was to block out everything and just go to the movies.

Only now, well over 50 years later, has Mark come to remember that, as he sat in those darkened Spanish movie theaters, he felt comforted in his loneliness by the feeling that our father was somehow there with him, sitting in the next seat holding the popcorn, like he did back when he took us to see Dean Martin and Jerry Lewis movies in Bethesda.

Recently in my Uncle Bud's basement in Rye, New York, we found a copy of his first 8mm movie "The Scar." It's pretty hilarious, unintentionally, but funny nonetheless.

And *La Mimi*?

My sister said when she finally returned to our home country she was absolutely in awe of everyone and everything.

"Every person I met and everything they were all so effortlessly American. And I had absolutely no idea of how to be an American. I was awestruck."

Mimi never forgave my mother for trying to force her to be a *señorita*; maybe that's why she's perhaps the most American of us today. She's a happily married housewife living in Santa Monica, California, with two grownup daughters who have both been, like her, avid dancers.

She had a delayed response to the absence of my father, which manifested itself as an attraction to older men. One of these was an unscrupulous high school teacher in Madrid.

She is today ashamed by what happened.

This was during an era in which some of the male teachers in our high school apparently seemed to feel free to see the under-aged female students as dating material. As far as I know, the school administration either turned a blind eye or maybe even approved, there were rumors the headmaster himself was involved.

One of our former teachers told me at a high school reunion, rhapsodizing about his relationship back then with a 10th grade student: "It was a much more innocent era then."

I guess so. If can characterize what was for my sister and by American law statutory rape as an "innocent" act.

Today Mimi says any grownup doing what her teacher did back then should be thrown in jail. She says she saw him back then as father fill in.

What he saw in a high school girl more than a dozen years younger than him you can easily imagine.

This teacher went on to be head of admissions at his alma mater, a prestigious top drawer US university. One can only hope he didn't use that power position in admissions to similarly prey on attractive young ladies eager for an inside track to an Ivy League sheepskin.

Later Mimi married a really nice older guy only to wake up one day to realize it wasn't right, she had unconsciously married a father figure.

Today her second husband is actually younger than Mimi is.

Whenever I call my sister now and try to talk about Torremolinos she quickly gets bored and says it's all in the past, not worth talking about.

Our mother, the *Señora,* spent quite a few years in Madrid after we all left for college.

Then back in 1982 she moved to Great Barrington, Massachusetts, where she sold real estate until retiring to Santa Monica in 2003.

Had she instead bought substantial real estate when we were back in Torremolinos she wouldn't have ever needed to work. She would have been a true and rich *Señora.*

Hindsight.

She died of a sudden stroke in Santa Monica, in 2010, at the age of 92, at my sister's home.

One moment, she was cheering Rafael Nadal on in her not-very-good Spanish as he was winning the US Open.

A short while later, she was gone.

My father, the aviation inspiration, died at 69 of lung cancer, after years of smoking Lucky Strikes, and then, because my stepmother said it was supposedly healthier, switching to filtered Newports.

When I remember how he looked a few days before he died, like some hideous skeleton from a concentration camp trying to force a weak smile through the fog of drugs and excruciating pain in his Sibley hospital bed in DC, I wonder how those tobacco execs can sleep at night.

Me, *El Daybe,* I've been a pretty successful writer, first as a journalist then in advertising, but it took me a long time to get there.

On returning to America I, like my brother Mark, was surprised to find it very different from what I had imagined.

I struggled to learn things every American takes for granted, like the rules of baseball and football, catch phrases, TV shows, etc. It was like I had to learn a whole new culture and vocabulary and way of being that everyone else seemed fluent in.

I had to play catch up ball for so many years just to keep my head above water.

In many ways I felt like someone who enters a track meet, gets in the starting blocks and asks the guy with the starter pistol "Where are all the other runners?"

"They started two hours ago."

One of the most startling differences between the America I had pictured from so far away and the on the ground reality was in race relations.

My notion of that while in Spain came from Time and Newsweek magazine. I had read about and cheered on the freedom rides and marches, Supreme Court rulings, school desegregation and I believed my country was now in synch with the whole deal.

We were going to work together all of us, black and white, to build a new and fairer America.

That came crashing to the ground when at 14 I returned to the US to live with my father for the summer and work at a job he had arranged for me at American Aviation Publications in Washington DC on M Street.

In their offices, a kindly older lady named Fran took me under her wing, helped me fill out papers and feel at home. I sort of thought of her as my friendly office grandmother, someone so nice butter wouldn't melt in her mouth.

That summer, Martin Luther King was coming to Washington to lead a freedom march. I had read all about him and desperately wanted to go hear this great leader speak at the Lincoln Memorial. But my father wouldn't let me have the car, nor would he drive me the several miles to the bus stop.

"There might be riots, " he said. "And they could set the city on fire. You won't be safe, son."

And I knew nobody who could take me, I knew no one there, there was no internet to appeal to. I was totally alone and a friendless stranger in my own home country.

That week at the office, friendly Fran saw me looking a bit glum and came over and put a comforting arm on my shoulder.

"David, you look a little down. Is everything OK?"

I told her that I wanted to hear Martin Luther King speak on Sunday but wouldn't be able to get in to DC.

Just like that, the kindly grandmother look disappeared, her smile vanished and her dark eyes scrunched up tight as she spat out a question.

"Are you with the niggers!?"

You could have shot me right there.

I was shocked beyond belief. My whole picture of Fran, and America, shattered so instantly I could almost hearing the breaking glass shards tinkling on the floor all around me.

I stammered out some reply about equality and America and freedom, but Fran was no longer my friend. Underneath the kindly office grandmother was a mean-eyed racist witch snarling out in anger.

"<u>Are you with the niggers</u>!?"

I've wished so many times I could go back in time and answer that misguided lady with something far more cogent than my shell- shocked 14-year old's stammering reply. I'd love to calmly say:

"Why yes, Fran. I am with the Niggers. I am with the Hebes. And the Spics. And the Chinks and the Polacks and the Wops and the Micks and even you clueless Rednecks and for that matter with the Fags and the Dykes and the whole big beautiful ball of wax."

"Because you see, Fran, I am with the America that says all are equal.

And I will always be. Always."

Even though to this day the reality on the ground sadly still doesn't match with the harmonious America I had dreamed of in distant Spain, I still see no need to let go of that vision and work towards it. Progress may seem glacial but we are working our way there bit by bit.

It will come.

Maybe even in our lifetimes. Or at least in those of you younger readers.

When I was in college at Oklahoma State University and almost accidentally discovered I was a writer, I took that idealism and began to employ it in the world of journalism.

Our student paper needed an editorial cartoonist and, despite my crude drawing ability, they had no one else so they asked me do it. I'm proud to say that my tongue in cheek lampooning cartoons of the administration and its blatant hypocrisy so riled up the Board of Regents they forced our hapless editor Jennifer Lamb to fire me.

"Sorry, David. The regents say there will be no more cartoons from you."

I believe the then Dean of the Journalism school saw something special in me that the Regents did not. With his recommendation and my good grades I transferred to the best undergrad J-school in the country at the University of Missouri.

After graduation I pursued the path of a journalist till I got to what I had seen as one of my goals: the Associated Press in New York's Rockefeller Center.

Getting temporary work at AP gave me enough of a taste of big league journalism to make me realize something really surprising: I didn't find journalism creative enough, it didn't satisfy me.

I didn't go to work energized and happy.

So I tried advertising. And, though I had to struggle for years to get a real break, that was more my cup of tea.

You've probably seen my work on TV many times for products ranging from Pepsi to AT&T, GE and DuPont Stainmaster.

I wrote the tagline "Grab Life By the Horns" that Dodge used for years and you saw on posters in most every major US sports stadium.

I also wrote the TV spot that brought Ray Charles to Diet Pepsi and, on the set of that commercial, improvised the tag line "Now That's the Right One, Baby, " which spawned a highly successful campaign that lasted years.

Lately, I am semi-retired from advertising and work sporadically freelance.

I've started to write other things like this book, short movies I direct and an unfinished screenplay about flying and World War II.

I managed to find and marry a terrific English lady. I think my years in Spain made me prefer a European girl: something about the Eurobabes lights my fire.

We have two lovely daughters who I've taken care to raise in one place and in America. It was supremely important to me to give them the sort of stable life, lived in one place with a set of solid lifelong friends, and the excellent formative education that I went without, including organized sports and other enriching activities.

I go back and forth on my upbringing in Spain. Some parts I appreciate, there was so much that was beautiful and special there. But, on the whole, I think you're better off raised in your own culture and without moving around a heck of a lot.

That said, I have to say that my time in Torremolinos and later years in Madrid have left something Spanish deep inside me. After over a decade of my young life sent in *España,* I feel there's a part of my soul that actually is *Español.* A part that gets excited when I hear Spanish music or hear real Spanish spoken. For better or worse, it rings a bell somewhere inside me.

Only after my mother died, have I finally been able to completely and honestly answer the question asked of me so many times over the years by other young people:

"Why did your mother bring you all up in Spain?"

The answer is: because over there it was the very best life my mother could possibly find.

For herself.

Beginning and end of question.

Recently I saw a terrific independent movie called "A Better Life."

It's about an undocumented and divorced Mexican man raising his son in Los Angeles. He realizes that, in this foreign country, his son can have a far better life than he has had, but that means that he, as a father, will have to make sacrifices and do without many things.

My mother was the flip side.

In Spain, she realized she would have a far better life than she could have ever dreamed of having. Parties, lovers, adventures, tailor-made clothes and she could afford all sorts of expensive things without having to work a lick.

But, in order for that to happen, her children would have to make many sacrifices and do without some very important things.

Like, for instance, their father.

Must not have mattered that much to her. You get the parent you get. Then you deal with it.

Today, I am also still very fascinated by any plane I see. I eventually learned to fly and bought my own aircraft, a single - engine Grumman Tiger AA5B I keep at Martin State Airport, near where I live in Baltimore.

Oh, and Davy Crockett, or Fess Parker, the actor who played him in the big Disney movie, I guess he did okay, too.

After a career in movies and on TV playing both Davy Crockett and Daniel Boone he retired from show biz to go into real estate. The Ex-King of the Wild Frontier also owned and ran a vineyard and resort in Modesto, CA. He died of natural causes in 2010 at his home in Santa Ynez.

But the part from the past I think about the most is Torremolinos.

What it was like then and what it has become today.

I worry about what the reality now says about human beings and so-called progress, and about what, in our innate craving for more of everything, we are doing to this planet.

Does our desire to live a supposedly better life and to possess more bright, shiny things really have to result in making what's spiritually beautiful so tragically ugly and pathetically cheap?

What is it about the human soul that, when we reach out thoughtlessly for glittering things, we so often carelessly destroy what's beautiful and come up instead with a handful of cold, ugly mud.

Other times I remind myself that I was fortunate to have had a chance to experience the beauty of how Torremolinos was back then, to get a taste of what was simple village life was like, to walk among its people like a villager, to speak their language, be a part of their seemingly timeless world, a world that in Torremolinos has now gone.

And, most of all, I wanted to share that beautiful experience with you. So I wrote this book.

I also heard and saw the old Spain plenty of other places while we were there this last time: in the happy voices of playing small children in a plaza in Ronda as swallows cried and swooped about; in small, sunny villages throughout Andalucia; on dark, narrow streets in Sevilla, driving past the rolling red dirt fields of olive trees in the south.

The charm and the grace that captivated me as a child are still there in abundance. You can't kill a spirit that strong just by taking a number of charming little seaside towns and turning them into glittering amusement parks for tourists.

They're gone. But Spain isn't. And never will be.

Spain is still *España* in so many ways. It's just that the quaint little seaside town that I knew is no more. And gone, too, are so many coastal towns like it throughout Spain.

So unfortunately today you can't hop on a jet and travel back in time to enjoy the Torremolinos that I was lucky to know: a simple, white-washed Mediterranean village back in the 1950's, like me, innocent and unadorned.

That unfortunate place rolled over and sank beneath the waves like the ill-fated Andrea Doria Italian ocean liner did all those many years ago. The innocent child, too, is long gone.

But old Torremolinos is still alive in me, and in my memories as an American kid, the ones that I've set down in this book. Perhaps it was the part of my soul that still feels Spanish that made me recall those times and write all this down for you to discover and enjoy.

Quién sabe.

Who knows.

I've done my best to recreate the Torremolinos that once was there and put it for you here on these pages, to make it live again the way I first saw it. As a sweet simple Spanish village in the sun, the Mediterranean gently lapping the sands, with a full grown man called Titi riding a motorcycle that doesn't exist down the old Calle San Miguel.

I hope this book has been your imaginary motorcycle. And now you've been there, too.

Torremolinos

ACKNOWLEDGEMENTS

I started writing this book well over a decade ago back in 2004. Having begun my writing career as a news reporter I saw it as something akin to that: a personal eye witness report dispatched to today's readers from a far away place called Torremolinos set back in the late 1950's.

This book is the time machine that can take you there.

I could never have persisted in this work without the encouragement of so many wonderful people: my lovely wife Jill who has patiently put up with so much, my daughters Rebecca and Emma who through me have a love of Spain and so many things Spanish. My brother Mark and my sister Mimi for contributing the stories they remembered and for their continuing support.

And thanks to so many friends from back then who shared parts of this adventure with us, particularly Nora Boren, who we knew as Missy Ericsen, and who generously shared with me lots of precious old photos.

Also thanks to Laurie (Riddell) Geary who has been a big fan of this project and encouraged me to great effect from her home in Gloucester, Mass. Like me, she took pains to raise her children in one place, with steady friends and in America to save them from the unsettling "Third Culture" experience both of us went through.

Thanks also to her little sister Ceci for long phone conversations about the past from Costa Rica where she now lives, today happy as an ex pat once again, as is her daughter.

Different strokes for different sisters.

And thanks to my longtime friend Merrick Gagliano for his help with Photoshop and cover design and for being my steadfast pal.

Thanks to all of them and all our friends from back in Torremolinos days.

I should also cite my mother Dorothy King. In her relentless search to find a more adventurous and carefree and grander lifestyle for herself she inadvertently exposed her children to a special village that captivated us and remains in my heart so deeply.

But the ones I want to thank the most are the wonderful and warm people of the Torremolinos of those bygone days. They opened their world and extended their hands (and in one case their fists) to the random children of "strangers" from a strange land.

Thanks also to all my Spanish friends from then and later. When I am in your company, *mis amigos*, or just in Spain I feel very welcome and *"muy en casa."*

A tip of my Davy Crockett raccoon hat to you all.

I have changed some of the names to protect reputations. In some cases I couldn't remember them anyway.

Can't promise every single word and incident are absolutely 100% accurate as this all happened very, very long ago in a land far, far away.

But I can promise you this: my memory is amazingly clear on most of what I lived back then and in my mind's eye many of these memories are quite sharp, like the point of a wild frontier Indian's arrow, flying back in time.

About the Author

David Mathis Johnson lives in Baltimore, MD, in the old port section of Fell's Point with his wife Jill and two cats, Lucy and Houdini (the son he never had). His youngest daughter Emma Johnson is an urban planner in Portland. Oregon, and his first child, Rebecca Johnson is a user experience designer (you'll have to ask her to explain that, Dad can't) based in Washington DC. To some degree all of them, except maybe the cats, have an affection for Spain stemming from David's tales of his early life there. As well as writing and directing short films, plays and this book, the author enjoys playing his guitars and *cajon* percussion in local hootenannies and cooks a mean seafood and chicken paella.

58533513R00173

Made in the USA
Charleston, SC
12 July 2016